IN THE FOOTSTEPS OF DANIEL LOBDELL:

A CIVIL WAR SOLDIER
IN THE
46TH ILLINOIS INFANTRY,
COMPANY B

BY KAYLA F. LOBDELL

46th Illinois Infantry Regiment
National Battle Flag
State of Illinois Military Museum flag collection

In the Footsteps of Daniel Lobdell
Copyright © 2025 by Kayla Lobdell
By Kayla Lobdell
Cover Design: Jennifer Morovic

ISBN SC: 9781645385912

All Rights Reserved. Written permission must be secured from the publisher to use or reproduce any part of this book, except for brief quotations in critical reviews or articles.

Images and text not created by the author are used with permission and are attributed to their respective copyright holders.

Published by Ten16 Press, an imprint of Orange Hat Publishing
https://orangehatpublishing.com

Dedication

I dedicate this book to my former co-workers at Freeport Junior High.

To Barb Padfield who first chatted with me about my idea and encouraged me to travel to all of the places Daniel went. She even gave me a packet of information about Vicksburg.

Also, to Gloria Moeller and Judy Birdsell who were the first to help me transcribe Daniel's obituary and gave me lots of information and encouragement at the beginning of this journey.

I will be forever grateful to these ladies for their friendship and assistance.

Table of Contents

Chapter 1: Daniel's Early Years on the Farm, 1841–1850s 4
Chapter 2: A Country Divided, 1858–1861 8
Chapter 3: Enlistment, Summer 1861 14
Chapter 4: Camp Butler Near Springfield, Illinois, 1861–1862 17
Chapter 5: Cairo, Illinois, and the Capture of Fort Henry, 1862 28
Chapter 6: The Battle at Fort Donelson, February 12–16, 1862 35
Chapter 7: Shiloh, April 6–7, 1862 40
Chapter 8: A Long Hot March, May–September 1862 49
Chapter 9: "Hatchie," October 4–5, 1862 54
Chapter 10: Corn for Christmas, November 1862–January 1863 61
Chapter 11: The Copperheads, Winter 1863 67
Chapter 12: Memphis and the Clara Poe, March 1863–May 1863 70
Chapter 13: The Vicksburg Campaign, Winter 1863–July 4, 1863 73
Chapter 14: Camp Cowan, Hebron, Mississippi, November 1863–January 1864 78
Chapter 15: Home to the Farm, January–February 1864 82
Chapter 16: Mississippi, March–July 1864 88
Chapter 17: Morganza, Louisiana, July 29–August 30, 1864 93
Chapter 18: Daniel's Final March, August 1864 100
Chapter 19: Barracks, U.S. General Hospital, New Orleans, August 30–September 19, 1864 105
Chapter 20: Mound City Hospital, Cairo, Illinois, September–October 1864 108
Chapter 21: Greenwood Cemetery, November 1864 113
Epilogue 115
Appendix A: Daniel's Family 117
Appendix B: Battlefields and Civil War-Related Sites 121
Appendix C: Historians and Editors 122
References 127

Prologue

When I was growing up on our farm, I occasionally stopped at Greenwood Cemetery, a few miles up the road to visit the graves of my great-great-great grandparents Joseph and Olive Lobdell and their son Daniel, my great-great granduncle. Daniel's ornate tombstone has decorative stone ivy and just below that, a hand holding a flag.

Figure 1. Lobdell Homestead 2013, Waddams Township, Stephenson County, Illinois

DANIEL H
SON OF
J & O LOBDELL
OF Co B 46 REGT
ILL Vet Vol
DIED AT CAIRO
OCT. 3, 1864
AGED 23 YRS
4 MS & 7 DS.

I asked my dad one time if he knew anything about Daniel. Did he fight in the Civil War? What happened to him? Did anyone in our family know anything about him? My dad did not think that he fought, and he was not able to tell me any information about him.

I did not take that as the final answer. I eventually began my own research and uncovered the story of Daniel's life during the Civil War in which he did fight. For over thirty years, I have searched for information about Daniel in museums and libraries; sent for his National Archives and Records Administration (NARA) documents from Washington D.C.; visited numerous National Battlefield sites; and traveled many miles through Illinois, Tennessee, Alabama, Mississippi, and Louisiana following in his footsteps. Everywhere I traveled, I collected maps, letters, articles, books, documents, and photos, uncovering many layers of historical information about Daniel's life.

Daniel Lobdell grew up on the same farm and in the same house where seven generations of my family have lived, including me. It is the Lobdell homestead on Flansburg Road near Lena, Illinois, where Daniel's parents, Joseph and Olive Lobdell, my Great-great-great grandparents, homesteaded in 1837. The land borders the Pecatonica River and has many acres of timber, limestone hills, and fertile river bottoms that for many years have produced abundant crops. This area was on the Western frontier in 1837 and settled by people wanting to buy land and then farm that land. Daniel's father and mother moved to this area of Illinois from New York and purchased the farm for $1.25 an acre.

On May 28, 1858, Daniel turned seventeen years old. America was in the middle of the fiercest controversy ever in our country —whether or not slavery should be allowed to exist and spread into the new territories of the growing United States. Daniel was aware of the growing national debate over slavery and states' rights, and when the Rebels fired on Fort Sumter and President Abraham Lincoln called for 100,000 troops, Daniel was ready to enlist and go fight.

This is Daniel's story from his life on the farm, his enlistment in Company B of the 46th Illinois Infantry, and the years he fought in the Civil War. He became a dedicated soldier in his beloved regiment—the 46th Illinois

PROLOGUE

Infantry—supporting and defending his comrades as they all fought to preserve the Union.

It is also my story of visiting many of the places where Daniel was during the war. This book is a tribute to Daniel Lobdell's courageous life and to honor his life, one that could have so easily been forgotten.

CHAPTER 1:
Daniel's Early Years on the Farm, 1841–1850s

Only he can understand what a farm is, what a country is, who shall have sacrificed part of himself to his farm or country, fought to save it, struggled to make it beautiful. Only then will the love of farm or country fill his heart. — Antoine de Saint-Exupery

Daniel Lobdell was born on May 28, 1841, in the same house where I grew up. He was the youngest child of Joseph and Olive Lobdell who were among the first pioneers of Stephenson County. Joseph and Olive lived in Brutus, New York, before they moved to Northwest Illinois. Brutus was situated near the newly built Erie Canal and provided the way for many to travel west in search of better land and opportunities. In 1834, Joseph and Olive loaded their two daughters and all of their worldly possessions into a wagon and traveled on the Erie Canal to Buffalo, New York, then took a cargo boat across Lake Erie to Detroit, Michigan. From there, they drove their wagon to Will County, Illinois, where they found an abandoned log cabin and bought land. The trip was over six hundred miles from their home in New York. In February 1837, Daniel's older brother John (my great-great grandfather) was born in the cabin in Will County. The land in Will County was very swampy and not good for farming, so that summer Joseph traveled further west to Stephenson County. He claimed land in Waddams township, built a log cabin, then went back to Will County and brought his family to live on what is now the Lobdell Homestead Farm. By the time Daniel was born in 1841, they had built a larger prairie-style house that is still standing.

If Daniel was like me, he spent his childhood on the farm exploring the hills and the woods. He probably also spent time fishing and exploring the

DANIEL'S EARLY YEARS ON THE FARM, 1841–1850s

Pecatonica River that flows through the farm. His father knew when he settled on the land that the river would provide fish; the forest wild game and trees for lumber; and the limestone hills stone for building a strong house and barn. There was plenty of long, lush prairie grass that could be harvested each summer to feed the horses and cows in the winter. With his hard labor and the help of his family, Joseph cleared the land and planted corn and oats. I grew up on the same farm, so I know that a great deal of time was spent just staying alive. The family had to cut lots of hay for the animals, cut a tremendous amount of wood to stay warm all winter, and raise animals and plant a garden for their food. If they were like me and my siblings, John and Daniel worked together each day on the farm doing all of these things.

Figure 2. Lobdell Farmhouse in the early 1900s after the front part was added. Daniel and I both grew up in this house.

My Great-great grandfather John was four years older than Daniel, and his sister Ellen was two years older than Daniel. They also had two older sisters, Frances and Elizabeth. Since Ellen and Daniel were so close in age, she and Daniel probably spent a lot of time together doing chores and helping their parents. Tragically, their father Joseph died in 1851 when Daniel was only ten years old. This loss for a young boy growing up on the wild frontier of Illinois must have been heart-breaking. His mother Olive and Daniel's older brother John kept farming, and life went on. I can imagine that Daniel and his brother spent a lot of time together at the river and in the woods, hunting, trapping, and fishing. They relied on each other for strength and comfort during times that were no doubt difficult for two young boys who had lost their father.

Figure 3. Map of the Lobdell farm, Waddams Township, Illinois.

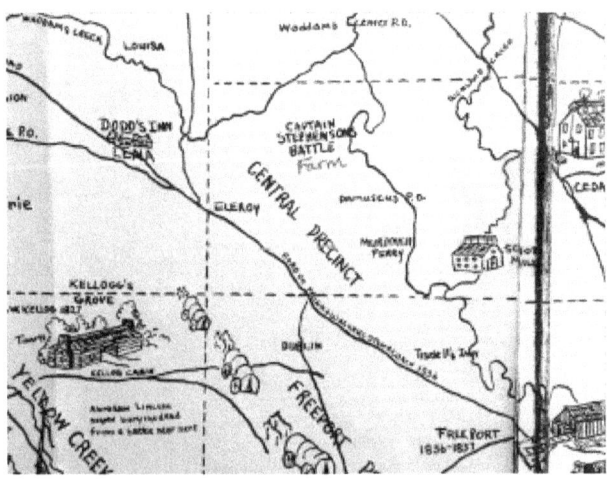

Figure 4: Map of Stephenson County, 1827-1853.

The farm was not too far from the Stagecoach Road, a well-traveled road in the 1800s between Chicago and Galena. When supplies for the farm were running low, John would make a trip to Galena to bring back supplies. During these trips, John would also bring back news about what was happening in

Illinois and the nation. The country was divided in the 1850s over the issue of slavery, with antislavery sentiments growing in the Northern states, including northern Illinois that had been mostly settled by people from the New England states. Southern Illinois, settled by people from the southern area of the country, was more sympathetic to the south. Slavery was firmly embedded in the south where there were many sugarcane and cotton plantations. The invention of Eli Whitney's cotton gin in 1794 led to a huge increase in cotton production by the mid-1800s and became our country's leading export, mainly to England. This increase in production led Southern planters to add more land and maintain and expand slavery into the new territories, at a time when the country was trying to gradually abolish slavery. Sugar was also in huge demand and a tremendous number of enslaved Black people were needed to work the sugar cane plantations in the Deep South. The enslaved died at an early age from the constant heat of working in the cane fields. When I visited the plantations in Louisiana, one of the tour guides said to us, "There was brutality in cotton, but there was death in cane." The enslaved worked in brutally hot conditions without enough water to drink and therefore would usually die of kidney failure at an early age.

On the Lobdell farm, the family relied on family members, hired workers, and sometimes neighbors to plant and harvest crops and do the endless work on the farm. Daniel and his family lived on a small farm compared to some of the huge plantations in the South. However, for pioneers in Northwest Illinois, it was a sizeable farm and supported Daniel and his family quite well. Illinois had rich, fertile soil and during the mid-1800s rapidly grew into a major producer of corn, livestock, and lumber. The land Joseph chose was not the flat prairie land typical of most of Illinois, but land with hills, river bottoms, and timber. John, his mother Olive, Daniel, and Ellen continued to farm after Joseph's death in 1851. Joseph's will listed farm animals and implements typical of a prairie farm at the time. They had cows, pigs and chickens that needed the hay and grain that was grown on the farm. The area had a good supply of limestone in the hills and lumber from the trees in the forest along the river and these were in demand for building houses and barns as more people moved to Stephenson County.

CHAPTER 2:
A Country Divided, 1858–1861

A house divided against itself, cannot stand. I believe this government cannot endure, permanently, half slave and half free. I do not expect the Union to be dissolved—I do not expect the house to fall—but I do expect it will cease to be divided. It will become all one thing or all the other.
— Abraham Lincoln, Springfield, Illinois, 1858

In 1858 when Daniel was 17 years old, news of an exciting event that was going to be held in nearby Freeport soon passed from neighbor to neighbor. The famous Senator Stephan A. Douglas would be coming to town after being challenged for his seat in the U.S. Senate by a newcomer, a clever young lawyer from Springfield, Illinois by the name of Abraham Lincoln. Like most of the people in the area, Daniel, Ellen, John, and their mother most likely loaded up a picnic basket, hitched up the horse and wagon and headed to Freeport on August 28, 1858, to join the crowd of some 10,000 people in town that day to hear the famous politician's debate.

Senator Douglas arrived by train the night before the debate and stayed at the new Brewster House Hotel that stood at the corner of State and Main Streets in Freeport, Illinois. A torchlight parade was held downtown and the next day the people were anxiously awaiting the arrival of Abraham Lincoln, due to arrive on the 10 a.m. train from

Figure 4. The Brewster House.

Dixon. Cannons were fired when his train pulled in, and everywhere there was patriotic music, banners, and more parades. Free barbeque sandwiches were served at the courthouse square, and people were eager to hear the two great men debate.

The Lincoln Douglas debates were the first of their kind and put Illinois and Freeport in the center of the slavery controversy. "What IF a territory wanted to free its slaves before becoming a state?" asked Abraham Lincoln as he took his turn on the platform, posing his question to the famous senator. Senator Douglas who strongly supported popular sovereignty (the people's right to decide) was a popular Democrat with staunch support in the South. He supported the Compromise of 1850 and the Kansas-Nebraska Act, both of which allowed restrictions on the spread of slavery, but nevertheless allowed it to continue. Senator Douglas's answer to Lincoln's question became known as "The Freeport Doctrine" as he replied to a boisterous crowd, "Yes, a territory may decide to free its slaves before becoming a state." Eventually news of the debates spread throughout the thirty-one states. Before the debates, Senator Douglas had the full support of the Southern Democrats, but they were angry about his response to Abraham Lincoln's question. These Southern plantation owners wanted slavery to be allowed to spread into the new territories as the country continued to grow.

What did Daniel think about all of the controversy? In northern Illinois, there were no enslaved Black people to do the demanding work on the farms. Children often worked from sunup to sundown alongside the rest of the family to grow crops, tend gardens, care for the animals, split firewood,

Figure 5. Abraham Lincoln and Senator Stephan A. Douglas

harvest crops, and fell trees for buildings—all very physically demanding jobs on the frontier farms. As Daniel listened to this new Republican politician reiterate what he had said in his June 16th, 1858 speech in Springfield,

Illinois, Daniel must have felt as many people in Northern Illinois did at that time, that slavery was morally wrong. Indeed, Daniel at least could sense a foreboding when Abraham Lincoln finished his speech by saying,

> *Either the opponents of slavery will arrest the further spread of it, and place it where the public mind shall rest in the belief that it is the course of ultimate extinction; or its advocates will push it forward, till it shall become lawful in all the States, old as well as new—North as well as South.*

Daniel could never have imagined what the country would have to endure in the coming years in order for the country to be "all one thing." Back at his home on the prairie, he understood that times were changing. His strong religious beliefs no doubt helped him stand steadfast in his own questioning between what was right and wrong, and like most people in Northwest Illinois he probably felt slavery was wrong.

The presidential election of 1860 was hotly contested, and the South was in turmoil trying to find a suitable candidate after they abandoned Senator Stephan Douglas because of his views on "popular sovereignty." The Democratic Party was split between Douglas who was on the ballot in the North and John C. Breckinridge and John Bell, chosen to represent the Southern states.

The Republicans met in Chicago that May and recognized that the Democrat's turmoil actually gave them a chance to take the election. They needed to select a candidate who could carry the North and win a majority of the Electoral College. To do that, the Republicans needed someone who could carry New Jersey, Illinois, Indiana and Pennsylvania — four important states that remained uncertain. There were plenty of potential candidates, but in the end, Abraham Lincoln had emerged as the best choice. Lincoln had become the symbol of the frontier, hard work, the self-made man and the American dream. His debates with Douglas had made him a national figure and the publication of those debates in early 1860 made him even better known. After the third ballot, he had the nomination for President.

With four candidates in the field, Lincoln received only 40% of the popular vote and 180 electoral votes — enough to narrowly win the crowded election. This meant that 60% of the voters selected someone other than Lincoln. With the results tallied, the question was, would the South accept the outcome? A few weeks after the election, South Carolina seceded from the Union.

(UShistory.org)

When I was visiting my cousins in Camden, Tennessee, I was reading the History of Benton County and was amazed that Abraham Lincoln did not receive a single vote in the 1860 election. In fact, he was not even on the ballot! It surprised me, although it  should not have, but it really highlighted how divided the country was during that time. Abraham Lincoln was part of the new "Black Republican" party, and many people in the country hated him! To Southerners, The War Between the States or "The Late Unpleasantness" as my cousin in New Orleans called it, the Southern states seceded and fought because of the election of Abraham Lincoln, because of disagreements over state's rights, and because the North imposed unpopular tariffs. Moreover, as one Rebel soldier answered when asked by a Union soldier why they were fighting, "because you are here." They were fighting to defend their homes and their heritage.

After the election, tensions mounted in Congress as politicians tried to decide whether to allow South Carolina and the other states to secede peacefully. President Lincoln was determined to save the Union but would not use force to keep the states in the Union. He did however hold fast that he would support protecting federal forts. By January 1861, more states seceded, and on February 4, 1861, these states held a convention in Montgomery, Alabama where Jefferson Davis was elected President of the Confederate States of America.

Alexander H. Stephens, a former Congressman from Georgia, who was elected Vice President of the Confederacy, spoke of his views on slavery and the superiority of the white race in his "Cornerstone Speech" in Savannah, Georgia in March of 1861:

> *Our new government is founded upon exactly the opposite idea; its foundations are laid, its corner-stone rests, upon the great truth that the negro is not equal to the white man; that slavery subordination to the superior race is his natural and normal condition. This, our new government, is the first, in the history of the world, based upon this great physical, philosophical, and moral truth.*
>
> (civilwarcauses.org/stephens)

On April 12, 1861, the Rebels fired on federal Fort Sumter in the Charlestown Harbor. Thirty-four hours later, the soldiers surrendered the fort, and the Civil War began. A little over a month later, on May 23, 1861, Daniel Lobdell celebrated his 20th birthday at the farm and was the age of the majority of the soldiers who fought in the Civil War.

A COUNTRY DIVIDED, 1858–1861

CHAPTER 3:
Enlistment, Summer 1861

Wars may be fought with weapons, but they are won by men. It is the spirit of men who follow and of the man who leads that gains the victory.
— George S. Patton

President Abraham Lincoln put out a call to all loyal states for 75,000 troops in April 1861. Why did Daniel decide to go fight and not his older brother John, my third great grandfather? John did register when the draft was in place in 1863, but in the summer of 1861, the brothers must have decided that it would be best for John to stay and take care of his mother and sisters, as well as the farm. Traditionally the oldest son would inherit the farm and that might have been part of the decision. Incredibly, 72% of eligible males left Stephenson County to fight in the war, which left very few men behind to harvest the crops that fall of 1861. At the start of the war, no one thought it would last for more than a few battles. They thought they would go down and "whip the Rebs," and the war would quickly be over. So young men like Daniel were eager to be part of the action. On April 15, President Lincoln issued his proclamation for troops, and Illinois filled its quota within five days!

Daniel turned twenty years old on May 23, 1861, and he was close to six feet tall and no doubt very strong from working hard on the farm. However, he had not enlisted yet and stayed on the farm that summer. On July 21, 1861, he and his family would have heard of the devastating news of the Union loss at Bull Run. The day after the humiliating loss, President Lincoln promptly called for an additional 50,000 troops. The citizens of Stephenson County along with everyone in the North were shocked again when the Union was defeated at the Battle of Wilson's Creek in Missouri.

M.H. Tilden in his 1880 History of Stephenson County described the days after the two losses by the Union:

"The dark hour of trial" when the defeats "disheartened the men of the North ... carrying sorrow and mourning into many a household whence some loved member had gone forth to return no more."

Though faltering, "the public mind was roused to a keener appreciation of the dangers that threatened and the difficulties that surrounded the country ... and this call upon the people's patriotism was responded to by thousands who pledged themselves to the defense of the old flag."

By August, if not sooner, Daniel decided to do his part and go fight to preserve the Union. The History of the 46th Regiment includes this description of the active recruitment of soldiers:

RECRUITING THE 46th REGIMENT. Stephenson County at first started to recruit three companies, viz.: Co. A, Capt. John Musser of Orangeville, Co. B, Capt. John A. Davis at Rock Grove, and Co. C, Capt. Frederick Krumme of Freeport. Later Capt. Wm. Young recruited Co. G, and Capt. John M. McCracken Co. K; headquarters of both companies at Freeport, Ill. None of the above-named officers were selected because of their military knowledge or experience. They were recognized as patriotic, zealous and influential citizens, who would inspire confidence and respect. Early in Sept. 1861 these five companies were so nearly recruited that they were ordered to rendezvous at Camp Butler, Illinois, to be organized as the 46th Illinois Volunteer Infantry, to be commanded by Col. John A. Davis.

(Jones 96)

The newly recruited soldiers initially gathered at Camp Scott in Freeport, Illinois. This camp was located next to the city cemetery just northwest of where Freeport Junior and Senior High Schools are now located. It was also located on the land where I lived at 817 W. Chestnut St. when my children were little!

By early September of 1861, Daniel and the troops of the 46th boarded a train in Freeport, Illinois, and traveled to Camp Butler near Springfield, Illinois. He left behind his family, his beloved home, and the farm where he had lived his whole life.

Figure 6. Sketch of soldiers gathering at Camp Scott in Freeport, Illinois

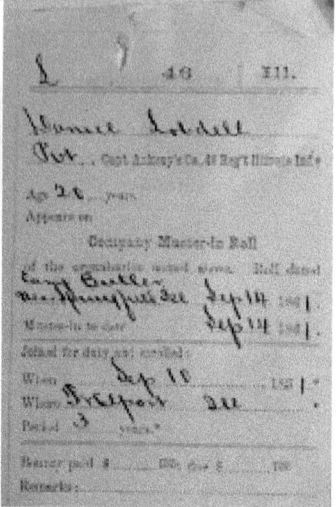

Figure 7. Record of Daniel's Muster-In, September 10, 1861, for a period of three years.

Figure 8. Illinois Central Train Station in Freeport, Illinois

Figure 9. Map of the Illinois Central Railroad-1855
During the Civil War, the Illinois Central Railroad placed its entire facilities at the disposal of the government. (Dayton 404)

CHAPTER 4:
Camp Butler Near Springfield, Illinois, 1861–1862

Patriotic zeal blinded most of these volunteers to the realities and hardships they were signing up to experience. — Gary Helm

Camp Butler near Springfield, Illinois, was one of the largest Civil War training camps for Union soldiers. At the beginning of the war, towns quickly created temporary camps such as Camp Yates west of Springfield. However, having hundreds of soldiers close the city and its citizens led to problems such as theft and public drunkenness. Farmers and townspeople complained about soldiers stealing their chickens and food from their gardens and orchards. Townspeople also complained about soldiers coming into town to frequent the saloons and visit prostitutes. Cases of public drunkenness and destruction of property were common. In 1861, Secretary of War Edwin Stanton and the state's treasurer William Butler selected a better site northeast of Springfield where there was higher ground, clean water in Clear Lake, level fields for training, and a close proximity to the railroad lines. William Butler was a personal friend of President Lincoln. In fact, Abraham Lincoln lived in William Butler's house in Springfield when he was just a struggling lawyer and did so up until he married Mary Todd. After the site for the new camp was chosen, Edwin Stanton approved the naming of it, Camp Butler.

I visited Camp Butler when I first started following in Daniel's footsteps. It is now a National Cemetery with 866 Confederate graves and 776 Union graves. The grounds are well kept with shaded trees and neatly trimmed grass. There is nothing remaining of the actual military camp except historical markers. The 46th Illinois and many other regiments rendezvoused at Camp Butler to receive training that fall.

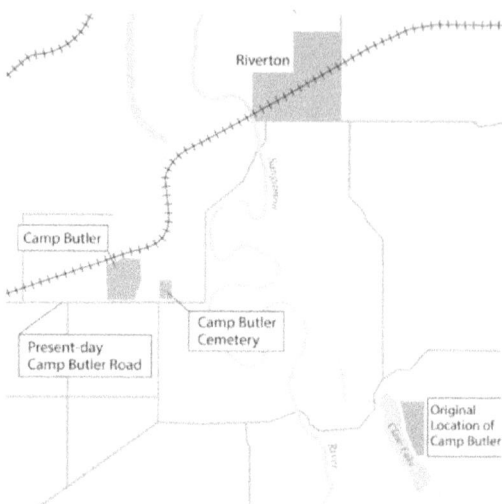

Figure 10. Map of Camp Butler northeast of Springfield, Illinois

Figure 11. Stockade at Camp Butler that housed thousands of Confederate prisoners

Housing was an issue with the thousands of soldiers gathered at Camp Butler. The Forty-sixth Regiment, while at Camp Butler, received a tent from the people of Freeport, Illinois. The tent was capable of holding 1200 to 1500 men, weighed 1580 pounds and cost $350.00. The regiment called it the chapel tent and Bishop Simpson delivered the dedication sermon. Later many religious meetings were held in it (Jones/Parrotte).

The 46th Regiment Illinois Volunteer Infantry was then, on the 28th day of December 1861, fully organized under the command of Col. John A. Davis of Stephenson County, Illinois. Col. Davis labored assiduously to bring the regiment up to a high state of drill and discipline with very satisfactory results. The services of Major F. A. Starring as drillmaster were invaluable because of his military education and experience, together with his patience and skill in handling new recruits.

Major Frederick Augustus Starring was a civil engineer and lawyer from New York who had received a personal recommendation by President Lincoln to become part of the Union Army.

 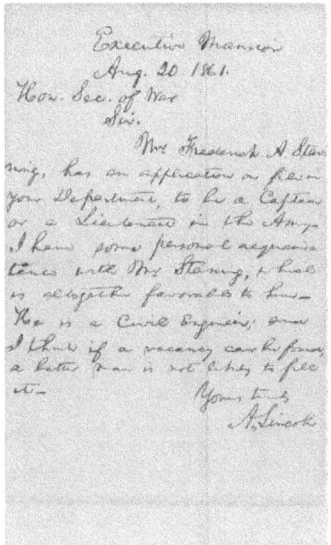

Figure 12. Major F. A. Starring

Once enlisted and encamped, a recruit such as Daniel soon learned that his time was no longer his own. Day and night he was under orders, a shift that required constant practice and discipline. Learning to march in step with a hundred other men, keeping a front and rear rank (two rows of men) in a perfect line and close together to commit to a heavily concentrated fire of the musket when given the command was no easy task for either the officers and drillmasters teaching or the recruits learning.

A good instructor is key- an officer or officers who not only understands the moves, but also why they are important and has the patience to explain it. — Col. James J. Dollins

The 46th Illinois, like many other regiments, rendezvoused at Camp Butler to receive training that fall. In 1938, Miss Emma Parrotte wrote in her thesis report The History of Camp Butler, many fascinating details of the history of the camp. She included the following schedule for the soldiers' daily program.

Figure 13. Captain Rollin Ankeny, Company B, Daniel's captain at Camp Butler

"Life in camp was very regular. At five o'clock the reveille sounded and all must rise at once and bound from the little A tent in which six men slept in straw and blankets. As soon as straw and chaff could be combed from the hair and the soldier properly clad, the line was formed in each company street for roll call. A half hour was then spent in "policing" camp, that is, in cleaning up the streets, airing tents, blankets, etc. At half past six the companies formed to march to breakfast, each man armed with a knife, fork and tin cup. Thus, they marched to the mess table, opened files to surround the table; the command "inward face" brought the company in line of battle in front of rations. "Touch hats"—"Seats," was next ordered and executed. The rattle of knives, forks, cups and tin plates and the roar of a thousand voices calling in every key for "bread," "coffee," "water," presented a scene of very active service.

```
      History of Camp Butler
    Camp Butler's Daily Program
             1861-1865

  5:00 A. M.   Reveille
  5:30 A. M.   Roll Call
  6:00 A. M.   "Policing" camp
  6:30 A. M.   Breakfast
  7:30 A. M.   Squad drill
  9:00 A. M.   Guard drill
 11:00 A. M.   Battalion drill
 12:00 P. M.   Dinner and rest period
  2:00 P. M.   Battalion drill
  5:00 P. M.   Dress parade
  6:00 P. M.   Supper and recreation
  9:00 P. M.   Evening roll call
```

CAMP BUTLER NEAR SPRINGFIELD, ILLINOIS, 1861-1862

At half past seven a tap of the drum called for squad drill. For an hour squads of men, nearly all the regiment, marched, filed, faced, turned, doublequicked, invariably holding on to the seam of the trouser legs, and soon became familiar with the simple movements in the schools of the soldier. At nine the guard mount, a pompous ceremony in which the Sergeant Major and Adjutant figured as great dignitaries. At eleven, Battalion drill for an hour gave all an insight into how much our company commanders did not know about war. Then dinner and some lolling about in the heat of the day; but two o'clock found the battalion again formed and executing many movements, the command and executions of which are long since forgotten. We drilled in Hardee's tactics, and then thought to be the perfection of simple direct evolution. We formed line, advanced and retreated, changed front forward and to the rear. We marched in close column, formed square; we charged at double-quick and retreated slowly as if yielding the field inch by inch, and we kept the little finger on the seam of our trousers, though the sweat tickled our faces and the flies tortured our noses. A grateful country never fully appreciates the services and sufferings of the raw recruit. Company drill of one hour was one of the most important of all, for here the commanding officers were supposed to impart to their men complete instructions, according to Hardee, in all the maneuvers in military instruction.

Dress parade came off at five o'clock. The grand ceremonial of the day, described by one of the wags of the regiment as a —"hard job o' standing still." At six o'clock supper and then the play spell of the day. Usually a circus was organized and the athletes of the regiment vied with each other, while the wags made the welkin ring with their drolleries. As darkness stole on the noise subsided into a hum of conversation in the tents, or the singing of plaintive songs, for the hallowing influence of eve steals over the rough soldier as well as the sentimental poet.

At nine o'clock the tattoo was beaten, the evening roll called, then camp was in slumber. Boots and shoes for pillows, straw and a blanket, worse than a white horse in coat-shedding time, made us comfortable beds, whatever our opinion may have been of them in those days of our callow experience.

> *A knowledge of military tactics and evolutions, well systemized commissary, quartermaster and medical departments are necessary, but arms and suitable ammunition are indispensable to the efficiency of an army. Two of the companies, A and B, were armed with Enfield rifles soon after going into camp.*

(Jones)

Figure 14. P-1853 Enfield rifle issued to Daniel's Company

Historian Michael Bub has written another detailed description of the training the soldiers received at Camp Butler: Marching and fighting, drill, and learning the Manual of Arms would become part of the daily routine for the Civil War recruit. Infantry soldiers drilled as squads and in company formation first, each man getting accustomed to orders and formations such as marching in column and in a "company front," how to face properly, dress the line, and to interact with his fellow soldiers. After some time spent exercising drill at this level, the company moved onto regimental level drills and parade. In most cases, these early drills of basic movements were done without arms or weapons.[1]

There were several different instruction manuals used in teaching these methods during that time, Gilham's, Casey's, and Hardee's each having both differences and similarities, which would prove troublesome later on. (Hardee's, which was the most recent published work, by Confederate General William Hardee, seemed to be the training manual most prevalent). One of the easiest commands in drill is "dress left" or "dress right," which simply means move over until you bump elbows with the man to the left or right of you, creating one straight and orderly line of men. The members then count off in twos, which determines how one moves in response to subsequent orders and more importantly, the position from which one fires his weapon.

---

[1] Brigades were not combined into divisions until July of 1861 or later, nor divisions into corps until spring and summer of 1862.

This would prove especially important when, in the heat of battle, members of the line may have fallen. "Dressing the line" effectively regrouped the unit into a concentrated firing force.

The result of this would be that these men would be able to move fluidly as one body. It would become second nature for the soldier to go from one long line into a marching column of four abreast on command, to march at the oblique, to be able to pivot or "swing like a gate," and to change the direction of a front when hearing the command, "Company! Right (or left) wheel!"

Being trained in the Manual of Arms, (Hardee's Tactics), the men would learn numerous ways in which to hold and carry their weapon- there were multiple ways, all named to properly hold a rifle, (for example, Shoulder Arms! Or Support Arms! Right Shoulder Shift! Arms!), few of these obvious or natural- but only one way to attach a bayonet, with a complicated but fluid flourish with the left hand. While in a company line, the recruit is taught over and over how to properly Stack Arms! (Four muskets clutched and intertwined at the socket of the bayonets. They would be drilled and taught many times over the proper procedure in Hardee's Tactics for "loading in nine times". The soldiers would be given nine separate commands, following each command, they executed a specific movement enabling them to correctly load and prime their weapon. Veterans often remarked many years later how they could still recite the steps of loading and priming, all due to the constant and continual drill the men were subjected to. The drill was important for the infantry for they used tactics that had changed little since the time of the American Revolution, or the Napoleonic age for that matter: Infantry fought close together in closely knit formations of two ranks (rows) of soldiers, each man in the rank standing side by side.

Before all was said and done, there may very well be a sham battle (as such the case with the 46th Regiment), but most definitely continual drilling in other soldierly duties: guard mount, bayonet drill, as well as skirmish drill. It would only end when the battle started and even then, in the lull of fighting, drilling and soldier life would continue. Sadly, some regiments would only be afforded a meager three weeks of rigorous drilling before being thrown into the din of battle. The remainder of the training would occur on the battlefield.

On account of changes from home life to that of camp and the inexperience of young men to observe the laws of health and use moderation in all their daily customs of camp life, many took sick and soon the regimental hospital had its inmates. The first death in camp of the companies then in rendezvous was Joseph McGinnis, Co. B, Sept. 28, 1861. Measles made its appearance at Camp Butler sometime early in the fall, and for lack of proper shelter much suffering was experienced. (Jones)

Joseph McGinnis

At Camp Butler, Daniel would have received his uniform and equipment. The uniforms were made of wool, and each infantryman wore a belt set with a cartridge box and sling, cap box, and bayonet scabbard. The leather cartridge box held forty cartridges, paper tubes filled with a Minié ball and black powder issued in small packs of ten. Each cartridge box also had a small pouch for a cleaning kit. The cap box, a small leather pouch worn on the front of the belt, held percussion caps, which had to be handled carefully because they were also very explosive. Soldiers carried a bayonet in a black leather scabbard on their left hip and of utmost importance was their canteen. Illinois issued a simple drum canteen to the soldiers that was covered with bluish-grey wool and suspended from a strap that usually had a colorful striped pattern woven into it.

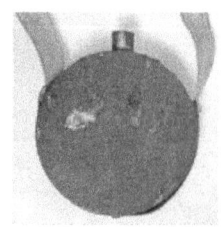

They received a cotton or canvas haversack, blanket, canteen, tin cup, plate, knife, fork and spoon. Union canteens were superior to most Confederate-made canteens. The body of the canteen was made of two pieces of tin with a pewter spout and cork carried over the shoulder on a leather or cloth strap. The body of the canteen was covered with a cotton and wool cloth which, when wet, would help keep the water cool.

(Armyheritage.org)

CAMP BUTLER NEAR SPRINGFIELD, ILLINOIS, 1861–1862

Figure 15. Soldiers of the 46th Illinois, Captain John Musser and his brothers James, Benjamin, and Charles

Daniel Lobdell and his comrades were now trained, equipped, and ready to go fight to defend the Union. The soldiers on both sides were fighting to protect their families, their homes, their communities, their states, their government, and their way of life. More importantly, however, they fought for each other. In September, Daniel, along with all of the other soldiers of the 46th Illinois, was ready to go join Ulysses S. Grant's Army of the Tennessee.

Organization of the Army: A Regiment was an Army organizational unit that included approximately 1,000 men during the early part of the war, at full strength. Usually commanded by a Colonel, a regiment includes ten smaller units called Companies, identified by letter from A through K,

Figure 16. Barracks and stockade at Camp Butler, Springfield, Illinois

omitting J. Companies were commanded by Captains, supported by three Lieutenants, five Sergeants, eight Corporals, and included 72 Privates.

As they were assigned to field commands, four Regiments were combined into a Brigade, three or four Brigades might then be combined into a Division, and three or four Divisions would later be combined into a Corps. An Army, such as the Army of the Potomac, would be composed of three or more Corps. Organizations, at all levels, would be realigned from time to time to satisfy the needs of the situation.

(Ohland)

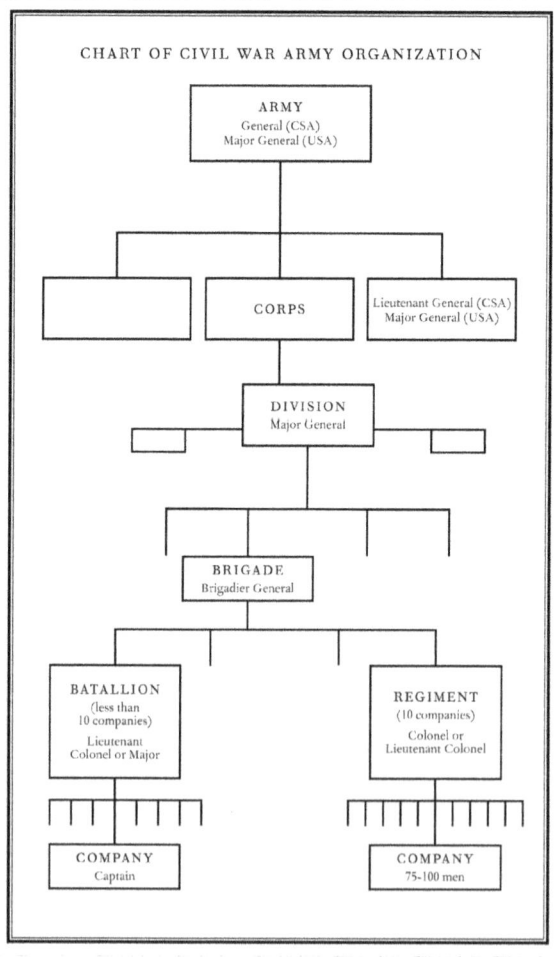

CAMP BUTLER NEAR SPRINGFIELD, ILLINOIS, 1861–1862

Leader of the 46th Illinois

Colonel John A. Davis was in command of the 46th Illinois Infantry at the time and was well known and loved by the soldiers of the 46th and by the people of Northwest Illinois. The regimental history includes this beautiful description of Colonel Davis:

> ...so well versed in the history of his country, so deeply read in political science, so intimate with all the branches of knowledge. Colonel Davis was one of those farmers who have raised themselves to positions of honor by their own efforts. Well read, industrious, active and energetic, he was the chosen leader in his party and often held positions of honor and trust. As a member of the legislature, he was known throughout the state; among his constituents no man was more popular than he. In the second place, John Davis was a man illumined by the ideal, inspired by the poets. He lived on the highlands where reformers dwell. He breathed the atmosphere of poetry. Shelley, the immortal child, Burns, the minstrel of democracy, the lyrist of common life, Whittier and Longfellow, were his favorites and familiars. The former, I am told, represented his first love and greatest joy. "The Cloud" and "The Sky Lark" and "The West Wind," which Shelley saw, felt and heard, hung over the Illinois farms, sang in the Illinois trees and swept over the Illinois prairies when farmer John Davis plowed corn or harvested the golden grain.

Figure 17. Colonel John A. Davis

(Jones)

CHAPTER 5:
Cairo, Illinois, and the Capture of Fort Henry, 1862

We stepped off the cars and wanted to step back on again, for Cairo was a wretched, flat morass, strewn with fallen timber. The day we arrived, infantry volunteers mutinied over bad bread and burned down a guardhouse.

Journal of a Cavalry Bugler

On February 11, 1862, Daniel Lobdell and the soldiers of the 46th Illinois left Camp Butler by train and traveled to Cairo, Illinois. Fortunately, the 46th Illinois did not stay long as they had received orders to join General Grant at Fort Donelson.

Figure 18. Fort Defiance at Cairo along the Ohio River during the Civil War

CAIRO, ILLINOIS, AND THE CAPTURE OF FORT HENRY, 1862

Figure 19. Point Park in 2017. The Ohio River on the left flows into the Mississippi River on the right.

Cairo (pronounced CARE o) was described by the New York Times in 1861 as the "Gibraltar of the West." It is located at the southern tip of Illinois at the confluence of the Ohio and Mississippi Rivers. The Illinois Central Railroad also ran through the town, and by June 1861 it was the strategic headquarters of Brigadier General Grant and 12,000 Union Soldiers.

Figure 20. Generals Ulysses S. Grant and John A. McClernand standing on the steps in the center of Cairo's post office in 1861

Ulysses S. Grant was a quiet, unassuming man, and his troops loved him. At Cairo in 1861, he was biding his time while the political squabbling in Washington continued. Grant was a graduate of West Point and a veteran of the Mexican War. When he resigned from the army in 1854, he did not have much success in the endeavors he tried. When the war broke out, he was an unknown clerk in his father's leather goods store in Galena, Illinois.

Some of my early research began in Cairo, Illinois, which today is a poor, forgotten town. Some people warned me to not drive through the town after dark! The Cairo Public Library is one of the few beautiful buildings still remaining and I stopped in to search for information and spent time talking to the librarians about their town.

The war in the West was a battle for control of the rivers, the highways of the country in the 1860s. Author Benjamin Franklin Cooling in his book explains:

> *What should have been understood by everyone at the time was the central feature of rivers to the way of life in the Heartland. Waterways, not roads or railroads, conditioned how people communicated, traded, and survived in the Great Valley of Mid-America. Tributary streams, such as the Tennessee and Cumberland, fed the mighty Ohio and Mississippi*

economically and politically, as much as they did geographically or naturally. Cotton was not king in this section, but rather bowed to grain, tobacco, pork, timber, and iron. Carried by steamboat and traded in the North for goods and services beneficial to the South's agrarian system, these commodities forged linkages between sections of the Heartland. Because of the rivers and trade, Tennesseans and Kentuckians had more cultural, economic, and even blood ties with people north of the Ohio than they did with those of the Deep South. Forts Henry and Donelson were constructed to guard the water passages but ironically became roadblocks to the one potential avenue for compromise or reconciliation.

(Cooling, p. xii)

The Army and Navy commanders Grant and Foote in the Western front were described by noted historian James McPherson in his Pulitzer Prize-winning book *The Battle Cry of Freedom* as follows:

The God-fearing, tee totaling, antislavery Connecticut Yankee Flag-Officer Andrew H. Foot; and Brigadier-General Ulysses S. Grant, who may have feared God but was indifferent toward slavery and not noted for abstinence. It was lucky for the North that Grant and Foote worked well together, because the institutional arrangements for army-navy cooperation left much to be desired.

(McPherson, 392.)

Indeed, there was a great deal of political posturing during the war between army officers and government officials, many of whom had been comrades at West Point, in the Mexican War, or both.

The Western Flotilla, or as it was more popularly known, the "Brown Water Navy", would be bolstered further by a War Department contract won by businessman James B. Eads of St. Louis. Eads would supply the Army with seven shallow-draft riverboats, all with heavy armor plating. Designed by Samuel Pook and built in shipyards at Carondelet, MO and Mound City, IL the seven city-class ironclads, or "Pook's Turtles", would be named for various cities significant to their creation: "Cairo", "Carondelet", "Cincinnati", "Louisville", "Mound City", "St. Louis", and "Pittsburgh".

https://bookwormhistory.com

Figure 21. The Ironclads-- "Pook's Turtles".

Grant and Foote worked together to capture forts aggressively and quickly along the river, thus cutting off the transportation and supply lines of the South and keeping the rivers open for the Northern Army. The rivers were numerous: the Ohio River; the Tennessee River that flows south to north and was protected by Fort Henry; and the Cumberland River, protected by Fort Donelson. The main objective was to gain complete control of the tributary rivers and then ultimately gain control of the mighty Mississippi River, extending from the free states of the North, deep into the Southern slaves states all the way to the crucial ports of Baton Rouge and New Orleans, Louisiana. The gunboats were extremely effective at Fort Henry and the commander of the Fort soon raised the white flag and surrendered. Many of the rebel soldiers, however, escaped to Fort Donelson where they prepared for the next battle.

Daniel and the 46th Illinois were still on the way south and did not know that they had missed the battle! They arrived by train in Cairo that first week of February 1862 and immediately boarded the transport steamboat "Belle Memphis" that set off behind gunboats up the Ohio River to Fort Henry.

Figure 22. "Moon River" Painting of The Belle Memphis River Steamer by Michael Blaser.

The regimental history includes the following description of the journey Daniel and the other soldiers took up the Ohio River on the Belle Memphis:

But before the boat reached the mouth of the Tennessee River, the joyful tidings came that Ft. Henry was captured. Our destination was at once changed to Ft. Donelson, Tennessee, in the vicinity of which we landed on the morning of the 14th of February. As this was the first steamboat ride most of the men had ever taken, it was much enjoyed. Especially as the weather was pleasant and the swollen river covered with a large fleet of transports loaded with troops going to the same destination.

(Jones 10410)

The map shows how closely the Tennessee and Cumberland Rivers flow side by side, and the forts were only a few miles apart. The 46th had planned to take the transport ship from Cairo to just past Paducah and go up the Tennessee River to Fort Henry. Instead, because the battle was already over, they were given orders to continue up the Ohio River to the mouth of the Cumberland River and go south to Fort Donelson.

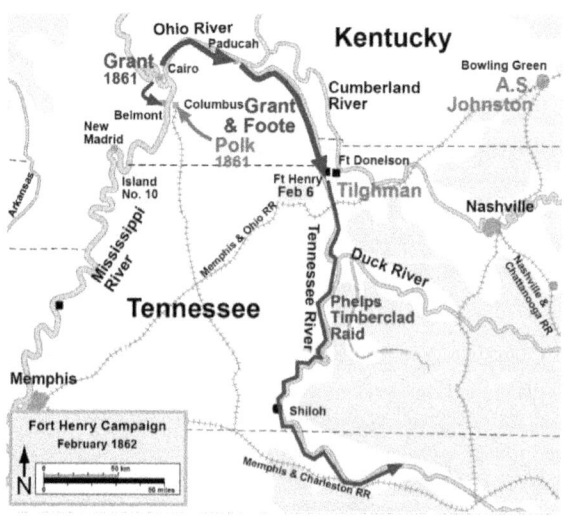

Figure 23. Map of the Fort Henry Campaign.

Fort Donelson remains a National Military Park site. Fort Henry, however, is gone. In 1938, the Tennessee Valley Authority built the Kentucky Dam on the Tennessee River near Paducah, and the water of Kentucky Lake now covers the site of Fort Henry.

CHAPTER 6:
The Battle at Fort Donelson, February 12–16, 1862

War is at best barbarism... Its glory is all moonshine. It is only those who have neither fired a shot, nor heard the shrieks and groans of the wounded who cry aloud for blood, more vengeance, more desolation. War is hell.
— *William Tecumseh Sherman*

I have visited Fort Donelson in Tennessee many times and each time, I have learned many interesting details of the battle. The view of the Cumberland River is beautiful, the earthworks are well preserved, and the cabins, cannons, monuments, and historical buildings are all well-kept and interesting.

Figure 24. Cumberland River at Fort Donelson, Dover, Tennessee.

Fort Donelson is on higher ground than Fort Henry, and with the fortified earthworks and 12,000 soldiers, the Confederates were more prepared to defend this fort. This battle would be the first for Daniel and the 46th Illinois. They would "see the elephant!" and experience battle for the first time. There

Figure 25. The earthworks that were built in the 1860s are remarkably intact. This photo taken by Daniel Thurber for Bookworm History really shows how large the earthworks were that the soldiers and enslaved built.

were some minor skirmishes the day before the battle, but the major fighting began on the morning of February 13, 1862. Some of the Union soldiers who had to march overland from Fort Henry ended up making a critical error. The weather was very warm, and as they started to get hot, many threw down their coats and blankets to lighten their load. Unfortunately, that night a cold front moved in, and the soldiers were very cold, some even covering themselves with leaves to try and stay warm while others kept a campfire burning through the night. So where was Daniel? The regimental history gives this account of the movement to Fort Donelson:

> *The march to the rear of Ft. Donelson was a weary one. For lack of wagon transportation, the men had to carry rations, blankets and cooking utensils, in addition to their arms and ammunition. The regiment bivouacked for the night near Gen. Grant's headquarters. During the night the weather suddenly changed, and the shelterless soldiers found themselves covered with snow in the morning.*

THE BATTLE AT FORT DONELSON, FEBRUARY 12–16, 1862

The 46th was not called into action on the main day of the battle and instead held a position near Grant's headquarters. During one visit to Fort Donelson, the National Park ranger at the visitor's center spent some time looking through old regimental maps and was able to find the exact area where the 46th Illinois was located during the battle. They were camped near Wynn Ferry Road, and they again suffered through a cold miserable night on the 15th. One of my favorite parts of the research was to drive or walk and find the exact spots where Daniel was with his fellow soldiers of the 46th. I took this photo of the area where they were camped on that miserable frosty night in Tennessee. It is still called Wynn Ferry Road.

The next day, the 46th backed up the 1st Division after the soldiers ran out of ammunition. Lew Wallace in his report praised and thanked the members of the 46th for the heroic part they played in helping to capture Fort Donelson.

> *GEN. WALLACE'S ORDER. Headquarters, 3rd Div., U. S. Forces. Ft. Henry, Tenn., Feb. 28, 1862. Soldiers of the 3rd Division, it was my good fortune to command you at the capture of Ft. Donelson. Sickness has kept me from thanking you for the bravery you showed on that occasion. The country ringing with the glory of that victory, thanks you and its thanks are indeed precious. You were last to arrive before the fort, but it will be long before your deeds there are forgotten. When your gallant comrades of the 1st division, having fired their last cartridge, fell back upon you for support you did not fail them. You received them as their heroism deserved, you encircled them with your ranks and drove back the foe that presumed to follow them, and to you, and to gallant regiments from the 2nd division, is due the honor of the last fight on the evening of the battle of Saturday, — the re-conquest by the storm of the bloody hill on the right—the finishing blow to a victory, which has already purged Kentucky of treason and restored Tennessee to the confederacy of our fathers. All honor to you. Lewis Wallace, Gen. 3rd Div.*

(Jones 7257)

I took my four children to Fort Donelson and showed them where Daniel fought. My daughter Haley liked climbing on the cannons, and we had a picnic at the battlefield park. When I was teaching, our team of teachers taught an interdisciplinary unit on the Civil War. This battle is one I taught to my seventh-grade students while we were reading the novels *Across Five Aprils* or *Soldier's Heart*. My students always found it more interesting when I could tell details of Daniel's life in this battle and in the war.

Figure 26. Cannon at Fort Donelson.

When I taught this battle to my seventh graders, I had to do a bit of storytelling and use the overhead projector to show maps and photos to make it interesting for them. I included the details of the soldiers discarding their coats and blankets, then freezing that night. I also told of Daniel being there, which only slightly interested them. But it was the surrender that always captured their interest the most. Confederate Generals Gideon Pillow, John B. Floyd, Simon Bolivar Buckner, as well as the brutal and fearless Colonel Nathan Bedford Forrest led the Confederate soldiers during the battle. They and their troops had fought well and cleared a way to retreat after being surrounded. Then Gideon Pillow chickened out (as I told my students) and returned to the fort. However, both Floyd and Pillow feared Northern reprisals if they were captured, so they passed command to Buckner and then escaped, leaving him behind to surrender to Grant. Of course, Colonel Nathan Bedford Forrest was not surrendering to anyone saying, "I did not come here to surrender my command" and led seven hundred of his soldiers on horseback through the swamps and escaped!

General Buckner's headquarters were at the Dover Hotel on the banks of the Cumberland River, and it was there that Buckner surrendered to Grant. Simon Bolivar Buckner asked Grant for terms of surrender. Grant replied with his famous "unconditional surrender," which from that point forward gave him his nickname U.S. Grant. He established his tenacity as a leader who got the job done. The South was stunned and the North was jubilant, as it not only had control of the fort, but also had captured 12,000 Confederate soldiers! U.S. Grant and his army had defeated and captured most of the Army of Central Kentucky!

**Figure 27. Dover Hotel on the Cumberland River
Dover, Tennessee**

CHAPTER 7:
Shiloh, April 6–7, 1862

Shiloh: A Requiem (April 1862)

Skimming lightly, wheeling still,
The swallows fly low
Over the field in clouded days,
The forest-field of Shiloh—
Over the field where April rain
Solaced the parched ones stretched in pain
Through the pause of night
That followed the Sunday fight
Around the church of Shiloh—
The church so lone, the log-built one,
That echoed to many a parting groan

SHILOH, APRIL 6–7, 1862

And natural prayer
Of dying foemen mingled there—
Foemen at morn, but friends at eve—
Fame or country least their care:
(What like a bullet can undeceive!)
But now they lie low,
While over them the swallows skim,
And all is hushed at Shiloh.

(Herman Melville)

Southern Tennessee was warm and sunny on Sunday morning, April 6, 1862. The peach trees in a nearby farm orchard were blooming, the grass was green and the wildflowers were blooming in the woods. By the night of April 7, the beautiful, serene landscape had been replaced with the worst death and destruction the country had ever seen. There was blood, dead horses, splintered trees, and dead and dying soldiers scattered all over the farm fields, the peach orchard, and beside the "bloody pond." The entire country, North and South, was shocked after the Battle of Shiloh when newspaper stories and reports came out describing the horrible carnage that had occurred in the two-day battle. There were over 23,000 soldiers killed, wounded, or missing.

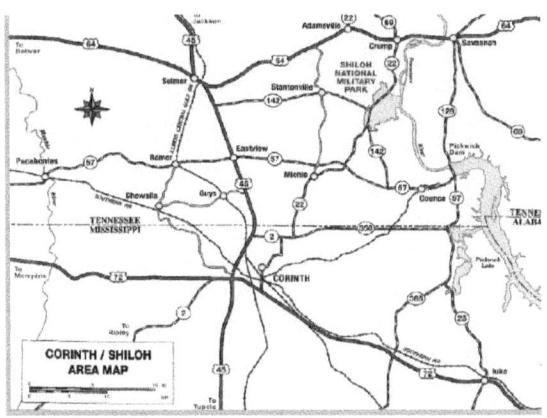

Figure 28. Shiloh Area Map NPS

One does not just accidentally drive past Shiloh National Battlefield Park and decide to stop. They must want to go there, to take the back roads deep into the southern part of Tennessee, just twenty miles north of Corinth, Mississippi. During my visits I truly felt a sense of sacredness while walking on the ground where so many died. The third time I visited the battlefield, I felt a strong connection to Daniel, more than any other place I had visited. Daniel survived the battle, but at Shiloh, he was shot in the arm. Perhaps it was not a severe wound or maybe he was one who survived due to the eerie glowing bacteria in his wound that was reported by many soldiers after the battle. He was certainly in shock from the roar of the cannons and the guns, the screams and the horror of two days of fighting.

In Larry Daniel's excellent book Shiloh, he describes all the details of the two-day battle from the denial of Sherman of the possibility of attack, to Confederate General Johnston's famous quote, "I will fight them if there were a million!" Grant and Sherman both had no idea the whole Confederate Army of the Mississippi was marching toward the Union camps at Pittsburg Landing on the Tennessee River.

Figure 29. Pittsburg Landing on the Tennessee River (**Author photo**)

The Union leaders had agreed that Corinth, Mississippi, an extremely important railroad junction, would be the scene of the next battle and were waiting for the arrival of Don Carlos Buell and more troops before they set off to try to capture Corinth. In fact, Grant was nine miles away that Sunday morning when the fighting began and was harshly criticized afterwards for the surprise attack. The fighting was ferocious all day on Sunday. By late that afternoon, the Union soldiers were barely holding on with nowhere to retreat since the Tennessee River was at their rear.

Daniel was with Colonel Veatch's 2nd Brigade and the following excerpts from Veatch's report of the battle give a vivid, accurate account of just how bravely Daniel and his fellow soldiers of the 46th and the other regiments in the brigade fought. (Jones)

Figure 30. Brigade Marker at Shiloh (Author photo).

EXTRACT FROM COLONEL VEATCH'S REPORT.

Headquarters 2nd Brigade., 4th Division, Pittsburg, Tennessee, April 10th, 1862.

On Sunday morning while most of the troops were at breakfast, heavy firing was heard on our line in a direction southwest from my camp. In a few moments the 2d Brigade, consisting of the 14th Illinois Infantry, Colonel Hall, 15th Illinois Infantry, Lieutenant Colonel Ellis, 46th Illinois Infantry, Colonel Davis, and 25th Indiana Infantry, Lieutenant Colonel Morgan, was formed in line and awaiting orders. In a short time, General Hurlbut's aid, Lieutenant Long directed me to move forward to support General Sherman, and to take a position near a field used for reviews, beyond Colonel Rap's headquarters. When we reached the field, the enemy was pressing rapidly forward toward that point.

A line of battle was already formed in front of us and a second line in the rear of the first was being formed on our right. I had but little time to examine the ground, but took the best position that could be found

Figure 31. Jones Field (Author photo).

to support the troops in front of us. An officer representing himself as acting under Gen. Sherman's orders, rode up in great haste and directed me to move my Brigade by the right flank and join to the line which was forming on our right. I executed the movement as directed but it placed the right of my Brigade on worse ground than I had chosen, though it had the advantage of forming a line of battle of greater length. (The order of formation of the 2nd Brigade was from left to right, 25th Ind., 14th Ill., Battery, 46th Ill., 15th Ill. In order to give place to Battery the left companies of 46th were massed, Co. K in front, Co. G. in rear of K, and Co. B in rear of these two companies, which proved to be a very great hindrance to the free action of the rear companies, as it endangered our own men and caused many to withhold their fire for fear of killing their own men.) The enemy now opened fire on the troops in front of us, which threw them into confusion, and they broke through the lines of the 15th and 46th Illinois Infantry, many of them without returning a fire. At the same time the line on the right of this Brigade gave way and left the 15th Illinois Infantry exposed to the whole force of the enemy's fire in front and a raking fire from the right. Lieut. Col. Ellis heroically held the ground and returned the fire with deadly effect. While cheering his men and directing their fire, he fell, mortally wounded. Nearly at the same time Major Goddard was killed, and the regiment, without field officers, was compelled to fall back before overpowering numbers.

SHILOH, APRIL 6–7, 1862

The enemy was moving another heavy column on the point occupied by Col. Davis of the 46th Illinois Infantry. The line in front of him broke and rushed through his ranks, throwing them into confusion. As soon as these scattered troops had cleared his front he poured in a well-directed fire upon the enemy, which for a time checked his progress, but it was impossible to hold his position against a force so far superior. Major Dornblaser was severely wounded, a large number of his company officers disabled and his color guard shot down. Col. Davis seized his colors and bore them from the field, presenting a most noted mark for the enemy who sent after him a terrific fire as he retired. I directed him to fall back and rally his men in the rear of the fresh troops that were then advancing. It will not be claiming too much for this Brigade to say, that, but for its determined resistance to the enemy, he would have reached the center of our camp early in the day. The field officers behaved with gallantry on every occasion. Col. Davis, Lieut. Col. Jones and Major Dornblaser of the 46th Illinois Infantry, each displayed coolness and courage in resisting the heavy columns thrown against them. Major Dornblaser was wounded and compelled to leave the field early on the first day. Col. Davis was severely wounded on the second day while gallantly fighting in Col. Marsh's Brigade and was carried from the field. Lieut. Col. Jones took command and conducted his regiment with skill and courage until the battle closed.

— JAMES C. VEATCH, Colonel
  Commanding Brigade.

~

The last time I visited the battlefield, I purchased an extremely detailed map, and even though it was raining, I walked for about a mile down a long lane, through the woods, and found the spot where Daniel and his fellow soldiers had their camp. To me, it was very moving standing in the spot where Daniel had been. As the rain fell lightly through the trees and the birds sang, I thought of many questions: How badly was Daniel hurt? Had any of his close friends been killed? Did he sleep at all? Did they have food and water? Did he cry? Did he just want to go home? Even though I will not ever know, I think that night he felt safe in the camp surrounded by all of his comrades who had fought so bravely with him that day. Daniel was only twenty-one years old and far from his home and the family he loved.

~

Figure 32. Site of the camp of the 46th Illinois Infantry (author photo).

The horrendous battle at Pittsburg Landing was called Shiloh because of the small, wooden Methodist Church that sat right in the middle of the battlefield. Ironically, Shiloh means "place of peace." After this battle both sides claimed victory, but more importantly, everyone realized that the war was not going to end anytime soon.

Figure 33. Replica of the original Shiloh Church- Civil War Trust (NPS).

SHILOH, APRIL 6–7, 1862

General Albert Sydney Johnston, considered by many to be the greatest leader of the Confederacy, was dead of a bullet wound that had hit an artery in his leg. The Northern press blasted Grant and accused him of being drunk on the day of the battle. Lincoln defended Grant when many wanted to get rid of him saying, "I can't spare him, he fights!" The war in the east was not going well, and McClellan refused to move his troops forward to fight most of the time. In the West, there had been victories and the war continued, in spite of all of the squabbling between politicians and harsh reports by the press. The news articles of the battles were detailed, and often the soldiers knew less about what had happened than those back home who had read the stories.

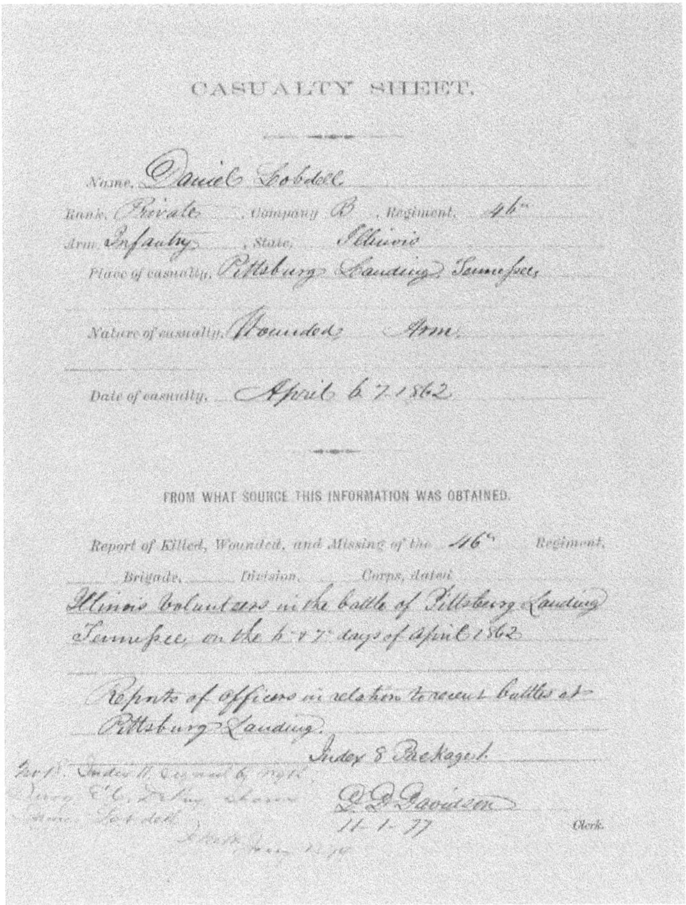

Figure 34. Casualty record for Daniel Lobdell from NARA.

Newspapers were not distributed in camp, as the officers did not want to lower the soldiers' morale due to false or exaggerated reports they might read.

After the battle, Daniel was transported to the General Hospital in Cairo where he recovered from being shot in the arm. By May, the muster roll shows that he was once again present with the 46th, which had marched onto Corinth with Grant's Army of the Tennessee while he was recuperating. After a long, cautious march to Corinth, the Union soldiers were expecting a fight. Instead, they found the town abandoned.

The casualty sheet shown shows a record of the treatment Daniel received from Surgeon Elias DePuy after he was wounded at Shiloh. Below is a photograph of Elias C. DePuy and one of Elias and his wife Lucy taken many years after the war.

CHAPTER 8:

A Long Hot March, May–September 1862

The air was oppressive even in the early morning hour, hot with the scorching promise of a noon of glaring blue sky and pitiless bronze sun.
— *Margaret Mitchell*

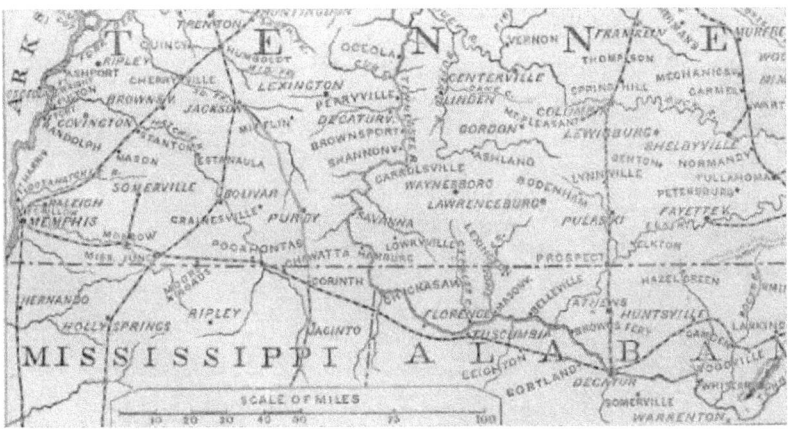

The 46th Illinois spent the summer of 1862 marching all over northern Mississippi and southern Tennessee. After the Battle of Shiloh, the Union troops marched to Corinth, the extremely important railroad junction. They found it empty. The Confederates had left, so they secured the area. Escaped slaves flocked to the area and formed contraband camps. On one of my trips, I drove around northern Mississippi to many of the places where the troops traveled that summer. Instead of writing a narrative of the movements, it will be clearer to just list all the places they went. Keep in mind the extreme heat of Mississippi and how miserable they must have all been!

May	8–30	Siege of Corinth, which included building earthworks and skirmishing with the Rebel troops still in the area. The Rebels left on May 30.
June	2	The 46th marched through Corinth
	10–11	Marched fifteen miles to the Hatchie River where they built a bridge over the river
	24	Marched to LaGrange "Collarbone Hill" and camped
	30	Marched twelve miles toward Holly Spring to old "Lamar Church"
July	1	Cold Water Creek
	5–6	Marched back to LaGrange in extremely hot weather. Men were "sunstruck."
	17	Moscow, Tennessee
	18	Lafayette, Tennessee
	19	Germantown, Tennessee
	20	White's Station
	21	Memphis, Tennessee

The distance from La Grange to Memphis is fifty miles, and the march was made in the hottest weather and over the dustiest roads. The regiment had been unable to procure new clothes for a long time and its appearance, when entering the city of Memphis, called forth anything but complimentary remarks as to its dress. Several officers had to substitute their last pair of drawers for pants.

(Jones)

They camped on the east bank of the Mississippi River and had picket duty from July 21–August 27, 1862.

August	27	Marched six miles to Nonconah Creek
	29	Went two more miles and captured twenty-five prisoners
	31	Returned to Memphis

September	6	Started for Brownsville, Tennessee, and camped five miles west of Memphis at Wolf River
	7	Marched sixteen miles through Raleigh and Union Station
	8	RESTED!
	9	Big Muddy River where they built a bridge
	10	Sent toward Bolivar, Tennessee but ended up instead at Hampton Station and Danville
	12	Whiteville to Pleasant Creek, three miles northeast of Bolivar
	14	Bolivar to Hatchie River
	14–27	They changed camps and there was a review of the troops by General McPhearson. But most importantly, their beloved leader returned to join them.

Colonel John A. Davis returned to the regiment and was very warmly greeted. He had been absent since the battle of Shiloh, suffering from a severe wound, which still troubled him.

(Jones 7891)

Daniel and the other soldiers of the 46th shared a camaraderie that summer, all suffering through the scorching heat of the South, endless marching on dusty roads and lack of fresh food and water. Most soldiers also suffered chronic, debilitating diseases. 254 men from the 46th Illinois died of disease.

The Civil War may have been a fight of brother against brother, but it was equally a fight of brother against microbe. The Union Surgeon General, William A. Hammond, famously claimed the Civil War "was fought at the end of the medical Middle Ages."

(Davis)

Nobody at the time, doctors included, understood germs, bacteria, or the need to sanitize medical equipment or boil water before drinking it. The food was also inadequate at times or even contaminated. Even worse, each place the soldiers camped, they dug open pit latrines and then covered it all with a layer of dirt at night. As a result, water sources were often contaminated.

> *Dysentery was the single greatest killer of Civil War soldiers. It differed from common diarrhea because it was caused by a bacterial infection that gave a soldier loose and bloody bowels. Both dysentery and diarrhea were commonly called the "flux," "Tennessee Trots" or the "runs," and all Civil War soldiers suffered from them at one time or another. As one surgeon put it, "No matter what else a patient had, he had diarrhea." Bacteria also caused typhoid and cholera. Typhoid was spread by flies that came in contact with feces or contaminated food, while cholera was caused by ingesting tainted food or water.*
>
> (Davis)

George Oscar Cooper, a soldier in the 46th Illinois describes dysentery in his letter to his sister:

> who the Boys here are all well with the exception that they have all got the Tennesee Quickstep they have no good water here and I think it is not a healthy place anyhow

Foraging by the Union soldiers was commonplace even though the officers would punish them at times if they were caught, but the troops were hungry, and the local farms in Mississippi often had food. They raided gardens and orchards, confiscated livestock at times, and often became creative in their means to avoid punishment as in the following anecdote from a soldier's letter in 1862:

> *Some of the boys will go out in the woods. They accidentally come across*

a hog. They order it to halt. It never lets on it hears them. Their guns go off accidentally hits him in the head, all of course done accidentally. He is then stripped of his hide-head, etc. He is then carried to camp and named a bear.

(Hicken, 81)

Author Victor Hicken describes more on foraging during the summer and winter of 1862 in his book Illinois in the Civil War.

The Illinois soldier, like his companions in service from other states, developed a fine sense of the dramatic with respect to foraging, as well as appropriate knowledge of the regulations under which he operated. When he was told by his commanding officer that he could take only the top rail of a nearby fence for firewood, he quickly understood that as long as there was any rail at all, it was the top rail. When fences disappeared, as they eventually did, the cattle roamed unrestrained—and usually into the camps of Union regiments, where they were slaughtered.

(Hicken, 83)

Reading the description of the endless marching of the 46th Illinois during the summer of 1862 and then 160 years later driving to some of those same places in Mississippi and Tennessee, helped me realize how incredibly devoted soldiers like Daniel were to their regiments. As horrible as conditions were, they would not have stayed just to "whip the Rebs." They stayed and marched on, fought on for each other. They were simply more devoted to supporting each other than to any cause. Most of the Northern soldiers, especially from Northern Illinois, had no experience with slaves or slavery, so they probably were not continuing the brutal business of war to end slavery, even though President Lincoln had issued the preliminary Emancipation Proclamation that summer. Ultimately, they continued on day after day to support each other in the endless fighting. It is safe to say, by the end of that summer, they were tired of "soldiering," and they all probably wanted to go home.

CHAPTER 9:
"Hatchie," October 4–5, 1862

Ask any living Federal soldier who participated in this charge, where he encountered the heaviest fire of the war and he will answer, without hesitation, "Hatchie Bridge"

> *The morning was beautiful, very calm, cool and pleasant. The stars in the heavens appeared musing sublime. Yet there was no moon to light us on our way that long to be remembered morning. The music from the bands appeared more melodious than common.*
> — *Sgt. William Newlon of the 3rd Iowa Infantry*

Gettysburg, Bull Run, Antietam, and Shiloh are all famous battles taught in many history classes. Hatchie was a battle I had never heard of until I began my research. One of the first documents I found was Daniel's obituary from October 1864. It was published in the Freeport Journal and was saved on microfilm at the history room of the Freeport Public Library. The obituary contains this line, "And fought on the bloody fields of Shiloh and Hatchie." Indeed, Hatchie was a very bloody battle, as were many of the battles that are not as well known.

In the fall of 1862, Confederate Major General Earl Van Dorn had a grand plan for his Army of the Tennessee to retake Corinth, Mississippi and then push the Union troops out of Mississippi and Tennessee. Thomas E. Parson, a ranger at the Corinth Civil War Interpretive Center, wrote an excellent article titled "Hell on the Hatchie" that was published in the magazine Blue and Grey in 2007. In it he writes:

Together Van Dorn and Price laid down a plan to re-take West Tennessee and drive the Union forces under Grant to the Ohio River.

In order to begin an offensive into West Tennessee and maintain a supply route back to Mississippi, the two men agreed they first had to neutralize the Union garrison at Corinth, The Small Mississippi town lay at the junction of the Memphis & Charleston and Mobile & Ohio railroad, the possession of this vital crossroads being the foundation for the Siege of Corinth the previous May. With the strategic rail crossing back in Southern hands, the army could then move northward, flanking the enemy out of their defensive positions in Tennessee at Bolivar and Memphis. The plan was exceedingly bold considering Grant's forces were almost double those of his foe.

(Parson, pg. 7)

Grant had his own plans and began sending orders to move his troops toward the Hatchie River and Davis Bridge, which had already been destroyed and rebuilt more than once. During September and the beginning of October, the two armies planned, marched, skirmished, and battled fiercely at times (at Iuka, Mississippi on September 19th) and continued to gradually move toward Hatchie. Daniel was marching from Western Tennessee with Major General Hurlbut and six thousand troops. The weather was unseasonably hot, reaching one hundred degrees at the beginning of October.

By October 4, 1862, Daniel was with the division camped at Bolivar, Tennessee. Bolivar was originally called "Hatchie Town" and was located halfway between Corinth and Memphis. The Hatchie River was a navigable route to the Mississippi River, and the north-south railroad junction made Bolivar a strategic position for both armies. Hurlbut ordered the men to cook three days rations and prepare to march. This order was no small feat as Hurlbut's force consisted of twelve regiments of infantry (including the 46th Illinois), four artillery batteries, and two battalions of cavalry, totaling some six thousand men. At 3:00 a.m. on October 4, they headed south out of Bolivar for Corinth, fifty miles away.

In the spring of 2019 I visited Bolivar, Tennessee where I walked around the courthouse square, read informational markers, and took several photos of the historic courthouse that was built right after the war. During that time, citizens also raised funds for the obelisk honoring the Confederate soldiers. It was one of the first in Tennessee to be erected after the war in 1873.

Figure 35. Courthouse and monument at Bolivar, Tennessee (author photo).

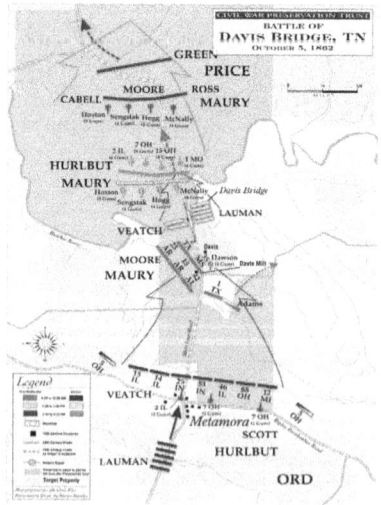

Figure 36. Map of the Battle of Davis Bridge-Hatchie (Blue and Gray).

As the troops moved toward the Hatchie River, Colonel Davis was in command of the 46th Illinois. Once they reached Metamora Ridge, the fighting began.

Figure 37. Metamora Ridge (author photo).

The following account of the battle is from the report written by Colonel John Jones on October 9.

At eight o'clock on the morning of the 5th inst., under orders from Brig. Gen. Veatch, the 46th Regiment took a position on the right of the 2nd Brigade, in the advance to support Bolton's Battery, two miles West of the Big Hatchie. After firing shots, the Battery took a position half a mile in advance, where they opened a galling fire upon the rebels, which lasted about three-fourths of an hour, when the word "forward" was given. The men all moved at the word and soon received the melancholy intelligence that our loved and gallant Col. Davis was again severely wounded by a canister shot. When I took command and announced this, the regiment seemed determined to avenge their loss, and soon an opportunity offered, for at this moment the rebels opened their first volley at short range, which was received with great coolness by the men until they heard the command to fire which they did and charged, driving the rebels over and from their batteries to the opposite bank of the river. Here the enemy made a stand, and confidently expected to repulse our force, but the word was still "forward," and on we marched at double quick, forming in line over the river. Here Sergeant John E. Hershey, color bearer, fell, wounded. Corporal Thomas E. Joiner, of Company "G," true to duty, bore both colors across the field and handed one to Priv. James Hobdey, of Company "I," who did it honor through the day. At this time Captain F. W. Fox, of General Veatch's Staff, took the front and called the 46th to follow him, when the regiment charged with cheer after cheer, until the field was theirs. In the last line formed, about four o'clock, P.M., the brave and generous Lt. Moses R. Thompson fell mortally wounded. I cannot close this report without special mention of Assistant Surgeon Benj. H. Bradshaw, who, unassisted, took the wounded from amid the ranks, doing even more than his duty; also, the officers of the line, who were all at their posts, fearless of rebel power, and if honor has been won it is due to them and their brave men alone. Herewith is a report of the killed and wounded of my command.

Very Respectfully, Your Ob't Serv't,
JOHN J. JONES, Lieutenant Colonel Commanding.

Throughout the battle, Ord and Davis were both shot and command had to pass to Hurlbut and Jones, which may have caused some delay and confusion on what to do next. However, by the end of the day, the Union troops had won the battle, and Van Dorn and Price escaped down a road called the Boneyard Byway and crossed the Hatchie River at Crum's Mill. Van Dorn and Price, having lost the Battle of Hatchie, gave up their plan to retake Corinth and Western Tennessee and moved on to defend Vicksburg. Interestingly, the next May, Van Dorn was shot and killed by a jealous husband!

The worst loss for the 46th Illinois was that of their beloved leader, Colonel Davis. The regimental history describes the loss of two of the leaders.

After the battle the regiment returned to its camp at Bolivar, Tenn. Col. John A. Davis and Lieutenant Moses R. Thompson died of their wounds on the 10th of October, and their remains were sent home for burial. Both were men of the highest worth and standing at home. Both entered the service with the purest motives, and both received their death wounds while bravely and nobly fighting at their posts. Their memories will ever be kindly cherished.

(Jones)

Throughout my research, I found it interesting to read many of the reports, letters of congratulations, and even poems written after the battles. It was imperative to bolster the morale of the troops who were endlessly marching and fighting. When the soldiers first enlisted, many thought the war would be short-lived, and they would go down South, whip the Rebs, and be back home in no time. Desertion was an ever-present problem for both sides, and the leaders did what they could to keep their men loyal to the cause and to their regiments. The poem below was written by one of the soldiers after the Battle of Hatchie.

HURLBUT ON THE HATCHIE.

The bright and gladsome sunshine O'er Metamora's hills,
has ushered in the morning, and happy flows the rills
Through meadows, banks and daisies and bright and lovely vales;
And silent flows the Hatchie 'mid peaceful hills and dales.
Hark! Hark! The storm is coming— It's the cannon's deafening roar,
Like the burst of Heaven's artillery On Hatchie's peaceful shore;
'Tis brave Bolton and his cavalry pushing forth amid the fray;
This bright and sunny morning brings a sad and bloody day.
Like the torrent from the mountain rush the patriot host along,
"Death to traitors is our watchword," from their serried ranks among;
Comes the sound, "God and our country from the bravest of the brave;
'Tis Veatch: "Remember Shiloh, boys, Once more our flag to save!"
"The gallant Hurlbut to the van. Where death supreme does reign;
Brave Lauman to the rescue!"— The call was not in vain;
"Our brave old State remember boys!" They dashed upon the foe.
The day is won; the traitors run; o'er yonder hill they go.
Farewell to those brave comrades who fell upon that day.

Poor Davis, Dodd and Thompson in death now silent lay;
Upon the field of glory, by Hatchie's peaceful shore.
They'll cheer their comrades onward to victory, no more.
Our brave companions slumber in the dark and silent grave.
On Metamora's hill top and where the cypress wave;
Here drop the silent tear of grief for our brave and glorious dead,
Who fell upon that bloody field where the gallant Hurlbut lead.

(Jones)

The following is a letter Colonel Davis wrote to his wife before he was killed at the Battle of Hatchie.

My dear Wife:

I have been sitting before my tent this beautiful moonlight evening until bedtime. The taps have been sounded, the camp is quiet and I am tired and sleepy. But my thoughts are with you and the children. Oh, how deeply I love my home and its household goods. I feel as if I could not retire until I had written to you. There is nothing new here; everything is quiet. It is good to feel that I can get a communication to you or from you in an hour's time should circumstances demand it. I am getting along well; I sleep well nights and thank God every morning when I awake that I have again passed the night in sound and refreshing sleep. I shudder to think of the months of long, painful, sleepless nights I have passed. Kiss the children for me, and know that now, in the future, as in the past, there is one heart that beats all alone for you.

Good night,
John

CHAPTER 10:
Corn for Christmas, November 1862–January 1863

> *When will this war end? Will another Christmas roll around and find us all wintering in camp? Oh! That peace may soon be restored to our young but dearly beloved country and that we may all meet again in happiness.*
> *— Tally Simpson, Civil War soldier*

On November 3, 1862, Daniel and the rest of the brigade left Bolivar, Tennessee, marching south toward Holly Springs, Mississippi. The regimental history reports that nothing significant occurred during this march, but it was slow going and miserable due to muddy roads, the emaciated mules pulling the wagons, and as always, lack of food. The troops were constantly on the hunt for the Rebels and set up camp at various locations, tolerated the tedium of camp life, and continued to move. One camp was in a cornfield where they stayed until the rain created too much mud, so they moved again. There was often a lack of communication with headquarters, frustration at times, and confusion as to where the troops were to go next. The regimental history gives a good account of what life was like for the soldiers during this march.

> *On November 30, they marched south toward the Tallahatchie River, and went into camp near Waterford, twelve miles south of Holly Springs. The enemy abandoned his works on the Tallahatchie and retreated toward Oxford. We remained in camp, in an old cornfield, which became extremely muddy during the heavy rains, until the 9th of December, when we changed our camp to a fine wood two miles south, where it was almost universally supposed we should remain for the winter; hence, on the 10th, our grounds were put in splendid condition, tents pitched in line, chimneys*

built and our camp christened "Camp Hall," when suddenly all our plans were frustrated by an order to be ready to march at seven A. M., the next day.

On December 11, they marched twenty miles to Hurricane creek, six miles from Oxford, and the next day eleven miles beyond Oxford to the vicinity of Youcona Station on the Mississippi Central R. R., where we remained until December 22d, when we marched five miles to Taylor's Station on the same road. Van Dorn having captured Holly Springs and cut off our communication, our forces marched North again on the 28d, through Oxford to Hurricane Creek, a distance of seventeen miles and arriving at noon. On the 24th the 46th Illinois and 33d Wisconsin Infantry, in command of Colonel Moore, left Hurricane Creek in charge of the corps train, arriving safe on the north side of the Tallahatchie late on the same night. (Jones)

Figure 38. Tallahatchie River in Mississippi (author photo).

The brigade spent Christmas and New Years near the Tallahatchie River. The camp was also near the Mississippi Central Railroad, an important supply line.

CORN FOR CHRISTMAS, NOVEMBER 1862–JANUARY 1863

We remained in camp until the 26th of December, making Christmas as merry as the means at our command would permit, when we moved our camp four miles nearer Holly Springs, between Waterford and Wyatt Stations on the Mississippi Central Railroad. Here the new year of 1863 was duly inaugurated with a feast, the best the country could afford, which was our whole dependence, as Uncle Sam's commissary had ceased to honor requisitions. The feast consisted of corn in all the varieties of style known to experienced camp cooks, except corn in the juice.

(Jones)

In nearby Holly Springs, Mississippi, Colonel Harvey Washington Walter, a lawyer and a Southerner who served as the President of the Mississippi Central Railroad had finished building his mansion in 1860 and did not want his home destroyed when the troops were fighting in the area. So he invited General Grant and his family to come and stay in his house while the war was going on. General Grant spent most of his time near Oxford, close to the troops, but his wife Julia, their son Jesse, and Julia's slave Jule stayed in the house. Because of Mr. Walter's hospitality, the town of Holly Springs and the Walter home were not burned, as were so many other Southern towns and plantations.

Figure 39. The Walter Place, Holly Springs, Mississippi (author photo).

In Candice Shy Hooper's article in the New York Times titled "The Two Julias," she describes Mrs. Grant's visit to Holly Springs with her son and her slave, also named Julia (and called "Jule").

> "When I visited the General during the war, I nearly always had Julia with me as nurse," Julia recalled in her memoirs. "She came near being captured at Holly Springs." Grant's troops had seized Holly Springs only a few weeks earlier, and when Julia arrived, the sight of the Federal general's wife with her slave provoked questions about her devotion to the Union cause. A Confederate woman who encountered Julia in a dressmaker's shop asked, "You are Southern, aren't you?" Julia replied, "No, I am from the West. Missouri is my native state." The Mississippi matron persisted, "Yes, we know, but Missouri is a Southern state. Surely, you are Southern in feeling and principle." Indignantly, Julia declared, "No, indeed, I am the most loyal of the loyal."
>
> Grant was at his temporary headquarters in Oxford, 30 miles south, when he telegraphed his wife on Dec. 19, asking her to visit him for the weekend. As always, she rushed to be with him, hurrying to the train depot with Jule and Jesse. In her haste, she left her carriage, her horses and most of their clothing in the house of Confederate sympathizers where she had lodged for the past three weeks.
>
> Meanwhile, Gen. Earl Van Dorn and more than 2,000 Rebel cavalrymen were racing toward Holly Springs. One of the raiders who attacked the town at dawn on Dec. 20 later described the "wild and exciting" scene: "torches flaming, guns popping, sabers clanking, negroes and abolitionists begging for mercy, women in dreaming-robes clapping their hands with joy." Capt. Robert Murphy surrendered more than 1,000 Union soldiers without a fight. He also handed over tons of military, medical and food supplies – and Julia's carriage – all of which the Confederates put to the torch.
>
> That was a great haul for the rebels, but they had their eyes on another prize: Mrs. Grant. According to Julia, "Some of Van Dorn's staff officers rode up to the house of which I had lately been an inmate and asked for me." Van Dorn knew precisely where Julia was staying, and it is possible

CORN FOR CHRISTMAS, NOVEMBER 1862–JANUARY 1863

that he knew Jesse and Jule were with her, too. In fact, Jule might have been an even greater catch for the Confederates than Julia that morning. Capturing Julia Grant would have pained and embarrassed one Union general. Capturing Jule at that particular time would have embarrassed the President of the United States. Twelve days from then, as the entire world already expected, Abraham Lincoln would sign his Emancipation Proclamation.

Although we know almost nothing about Jule, the slave must have been an object of keen interest to the free Black people she encountered as she accompanied General Grant and his family. Just as surely, Jule would have been curious about the slaves who fled their owners and followed Federal soldiers to safety, and about Grant's initiative to settle former slaves on lands abandoned by secessionists. As the signing of the Emancipation Proclamation neared, the trickle of slaves seeking freedom behind Union lines became a flood. Jule must have wondered at a world in which no other slave in the South but she could find freedom in General Grant's camp.

After their fortunate escape to Oxford, the Grants and Jule returned to Holly Springs, where they welcomed the New Year.

(Hooper)

Candice Shy Hooper provides this in-depth look at Jule, Julia Grant's slave:

> *"Jule had reason to rejoice on that Day of Jubilee. According to Julia, Jule was no longer a slave. "Eliza, Dan, Julia, and John belonged to me up to the time of President Lincoln's Emancipation Proclamation," Julia Grant noted in her memoirs. Technically, because the proclamation did not free slaves in areas under Union control, Jule and the others might have remained in*

Figure 40. The Grant family (Jule is not in the painting).

65

bondage even after that date, but a slave attached to Grant and his army of liberators would have been manifestly untenable after New Year's Day 1863.

Even after that date, Jule continued her service to Julia, most likely as a paid servant, as Julia lived with Grant in Memphis and then in Vicksburg. By the end of November 1863, Julia was with Grant in Tennessee, comforting wounded soldiers in his camp hospital. It is almost certain that Jule was with her in Nashville in January when Julia learned by telegram that her oldest son, Fred, was gravely ill in St. Louis. Julia and Jule and young Jesse quickly embarked on what proved to be their final journey together. "At Louisville, my nurse (a girl raised at my home) left me," Julia later recalled. "I suppose she feared losing her freedom if she returned to Missouri." We know nothing of Jule's life once she left Julia, except for one tiny but satisfying fact. In her memoirs, after describing Jule's disappearance, Julia wrote, "However, she married soon afterwards."

The tale of the two Julias reveals the complexity of the Civil War's social landscape in a way that the traditional image of brother fighting brother does not. One Julia was a slave owner and the wife of the general who defeated a slave nation. The other Julia was her slave for 37 years. The two women grew up side by side, but in two entirely different worlds. They traveled together nearly 5,000 miles, risking their freedom and their lives. They saw death, disease and destruction up close, yet they did not experience the same war. Julia Grant's war destroyed a way of life she had loved, but her husband's victories led to one she loved even more. By all accounts, no woman has ever enjoyed being First Lady more than Julia Grant. Jule's Civil War was a wrenching but ultimately liberating journey from slavery to freedom. She risked more than her traveling companion during the war. We do not know much about Jule, but we know she had fierce determination. Once given her freedom, she refused to risk losing it."

(Hooper)

CHAPTER 11:
The Copperheads, Winter 1863

"To maintain the Constitution as it is, and to restore the Union as it was."
— *Clement Vallandigham, Copperhead*

Daniel was part of a difficult march with the 46th and 12th Illinois in January 1863.

Figure 41. Map of southwestern Tennessee showing Moscow, LaFayette, LaGrange and Memphis.

They were guarding an ammunition train traveling to LaGrange, Tennessee. They slogged through muddy roads with emaciated mules pulling the train and arrived late on the night of January 13th at LaGrange. They then moved on to Moscow, Tennessee and then Lafayette, Tennessee (now Rossville) where they were on guard duty until the beginning of March. The garrison at Moscow at this time consisted of the 1st Brigade, 4th Division, and the 46th and 76th Illinois Infantry of the 2d Brigade, and two batteries.

(Jones)

The soldiers had to endure cold, muddy, challenging work that winter. Meanwhile there was deep division in the Democrat Party in the North. The Copperheads, also known as the "Peace Democrats" were speaking out against the war. They were extremely upset about the Emancipation Proclamation, fearing the freed blacks would take jobs in the north. They were anti-abolition, anti-Civil War, and anti-President Lincoln. President Lincoln referred to them as "the fire in the rear." In response, while at Lafayette, Tennessee, Colonel Cyrus Hall called a meeting of several officers. The following resolution was drawn up and written by the officers of the brigade in response to the Copperheads. The resolution was read to the soldiers in each regiment and voted on. Then it was sent north to be published in various newspapers, including the Illinois Journal and Chicago Tribune. — Colonel Cyrus Hall

The following is from the resolution printed in *The Illinois Journal* in Springfield, Illinois on Friday, February 27, 1863 on page 2. It showed support for Illinois leadership and military contributions by rejecting the peace negotiations of the Copperheads. It bolstered the morale of the soldiers on the battlefield and their families back home by showing the overwhelming unity and loyalty that the soldiers had for the Union cause.

WHEREAS, Our Government is now engaged in a mighty struggle for the preservation of the Constitution and Union, which should call forth the united, active sympathy and co-operation of every loyal citizen; and whereas, we have been grieved and mortified beyond measure by the wicked and traitorous course pursued by prominent politicians and Legislatures of the loyal States, and especially of our own noble State of Illinois, to excite a bitter, vindictive and dangerous opposition to the just means adopted by our State and National authorities to crush this monstrous and unnatural rebellion: therefore,

Be it resolved, That we have the utmost confidence in the President of the United States, and the Governor of the State of Illinois; and we do now heartily approve of the emancipation proclamation of the President, and that we again renew our pledge to stand by and aid him in carrying out every measure calculated to bring about a speedy, honorable and permanent peace.

The votes of the regiments were overwhelmingly cast in favor of the resolution, which bore resolute language upholding the cause of the Union. A mere three votes stood in dissent, and upon the resolution's adoption, the assembled troops gave voice to their approval with hearty cheers.

Figure 42. Colonel Benjamin Dornblaser, 46th Illinois.

Figure 43. Soldiers of Company H, 76th Illinois.

CHAPTER 12:
Memphis and the Clara Poe, March 1863–May 1863

Let us cross over the river and rest under the shade of the trees.
— *Thomas "Stonewall" Jackson*

On March 9, 1863, the soldiers marched via the Collierville and Germantown Roads to Memphis, Tennessee where they made camp close to the racetrack and fairgrounds. The regimental history notes that this site was a good place for their camp and for drilling.

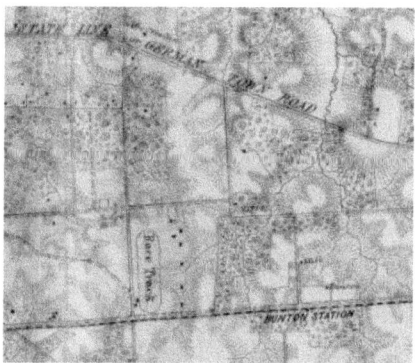

Figure 44. Map of Memphis Racetrack and Fairgrounds.

Jones writes of the movements of the troops while in this area:

> On the 21st of April, the 46th, 14th Illinois Infantry and 5th Ohio Battery were sent out to re-enforce Colonel Bryant of the 12th Wisconsin Infantry, who had gone in the direction of Hernando, Mississippi with a brigade and met the enemy in force near Cold Water. He then moved his

whole force again three miles south of Hernando and encamped for the night, as the cavalry had reported the enemy gone.

Colonel Bryant had captured and sent to Memphis about seventy prisoners and a large lot of mules and horses. April 23rd, commenced our return march to Memphis, where we arrived on the 24th, thoroughly drenched by a heavy rain. We met with no loss and the troops made the march in good time and in fine order. We remained in camp at Memphis until the 13th of May, when we embarked on the Steamer "Clara Poe," and left the same evening for Vicksburg, Mississippi.

(Jones)

Early in the war, everyone realized that whoever controlled the rivers would win the war. The rivers were the highways of the country, and supplies and troops could travel in days by boat distances it would take months to cover on foot. From the start of the war, battles for control of the rivers raged. When Daniel and the 46th prepared to travel to Vicksburg, they boarded a famous steamboat called the Clara Poe.

Figure 45. The Clara Poe.

The Clara Poe was one of six steamboats chartered by Commodore W. J. Kountz, who had charge of transportation by river of all of the Union troops and government supplies. Steamer Clara Poe transported troops to Shiloh, and now Daniel and the 46th along with the 14th Illinois left Memphis on May 13, 1863, and headed downriver to the next major battle at Vicksburg, Mississippi. They had a little trouble on the way. Tragically, Private Gottlieb Vohmer accidentally fell overboard from the Clara Poe and drowned on the first day.

> *In addition, Confederate gunboats fired at and disabled the Steamer Fort Wayne that was transporting the 76th Illinois. They were able to continue their trip and arrived at Young's Point at 8 P.M. on May 15, 1863 to join the rest of Grant's Army at the Siege of Vicksburg.*

(Jones)

CHAPTER 13:
The Vicksburg Campaign, Winter 1863–July 4, 1863

See what a lot of land these fellows hold, of which Vicksburg is the key! The war can never be brought to a close until that key is in our pocket. We can take all the northern ports of the Confederacy, and they can defy us from Vicksburg. — Abraham Lincoln

Vicksburg was originally pro-Union according to author and historian Gordon A. Cotton... "until they started shooting at us!" Both President Lincoln and Confederate President Jefferson Davis knew early in the war that Vicksburg, located high on a bluff overlooking the Mississippi River, was one of the most important towns in the country. Control of Vicksburg meant control of the Mississippi River, and whoever had control of the nation's main waterway would ultimately win the war. Indeed, the Battle of Shiloh was fought as Grant was making his way south in order to capture Vicksburg. However, as Grant found out, there was no easy way to capture this important river town. By the time Daniel and the 46th arrived at Vicksburg, a lot of fighting had already taken place in Mississippi and around Vicksburg.

I am very fond of Vicksburg, Mississippi, having visited on three separate occasions. Vicksburg National Battlefield

Figure 46. Illinois Monument (author photo).

Park is beautiful, especially in the spring and summer when the flowers are blooming. One of the times I visited, I had all three of my dogs along, and the park is very pet friendly. As one does at many of the battlefield parks, I drove the sixteen-mile tour, stopping at various locations to read the markers and figure out where Daniel would have fought. There are over 1,400 monuments in the battlefield park with the Illinois Memorial monument being the largest and most beautiful. It was modeled after the Roman Pantheon, made of Georgia granite and white marble, has forty-seven steps (one for each day of the siege), and cost the state of Illinois $194,423.92 when it was built in the early 1900s.

Inside are a series of bronze panels on the walls memorializing the 36,325 soldiers from Illinois who participated in the Vicksburg Campaign, including Daniel's name.

Figure 47. Bronze panels with Daniel's name (author photo).

After I toured the monument, I parked under a tree and let all three of my dogs out, first walking them and then tying them next to my Yukon to rest in the shade for a while. I parked by the historic Shirley House with a lovely kitchen garden and an even lovelier Southern lady working in the garden. She commented on my dogs lying peacefully next to my Yukon as I walked around the garden, and we struck up a conversation. We talked about the battlefield, and I told her I was traveling around the country researching the many places Daniel had fought. I mentioned that many people had been concerned about me traveling alone, and she said in her beautiful Southern accent, "Oh honey, they'll pick an easier target than you with your three dogs!" And she was right. No one has ever bothered me!

The Campaign for Vicksburg started in the winter of 1862, continuing on to 1863, and did not end until Pemberton surrendered to Grant on July 4, 1863. The campaign had so many different, interesting parts such as Grant's crazy idea of digging a canal; horrid marches through swamps and muddy roads; brilliant plans such as the midnight trip of gunboats sneaking past the Confederate battery; constant bombardment of the city by the Union batteries; newspapers printed on wallpaper; Union soldiers blowing up areas close to Vicksburg; and soldiers riding their horses up the courthouse stairs!

There were five battles before the siege began, at Port Gibson, Jackson, Raymond, Champions Hill, and Big Black River. Due to the Napoleonic style of fighting that was still being used by both sides, the battles were brutal, and thousands of soldiers on both sides were killed and wounded. In the small town of Raymond, the courthouse and a church were located just across the street from each other. After the Battle of Raymond, the Confederate Field Hospital was set up in the courthouse, and the Union Field Hospital was located close by in the Episcopal Church. The citizens of Raymond helped care for all of the soldiers and that remarkable act is portrayed on the stone marker in Raymond.

Figure 48. Stone marker at Raymond (author photo).

Pemberton retreated with his army back to Vicksburg after these battles, and at Vicksburg, Grant and his army attacked full-on twice, only to be driven back. It was at that point, Grant decided to have his soldiers dig in and lay siege to the city, for 47 days! A siege is just a waiting game to outlast the enemy, or as one historian said, to out camp them. Grant had his 129 cannons fire into the city continuously day and night and of course, all food supplies were cut off to the Confederate soldiers and the five thousand townspeople. They dug caves into the sides of the hills and waited and starved. Much of the town was destroyed, but the beautiful courthouse stood high with a Confederate flag flying mockingly atop during the whole siege. The Rebels had put all of the Yankee prisoners inside preventing the Union cannons from shooting at and destroying the courthouse.

Grant was determined to capture Vicksburg no matter what it took, and he tried every way possible, while the equally determined Pemberton and his Confederate Army resisted time after time. And then, remarkably, when the Confederates finally surrendered after the 47-day siege on July 4, 1863, General Grant told the starving, bedraggled Confederate soldiers to stack their arms, paroled them, and told them to go home!

Where in all of this fighting and chaos was Daniel? I had found his name on the wall inside the magnificent Illinois memorial in the park, but it took some searching by the park rangers on battle maps to find where the 46th was located during the siege. Their position for most of the time was outside the boundaries of where the battlefield park is now, closer to downtown. Daniel and the 46th were positioned next to where the Sonic Drive-In is now located! It was just so strange to drive down Illinois Road beside Sonic and then pull up next to the stone markers where

Figure 49. Illinois Road where Daniel and the 46th fought (author photo).

Daniel fought. There was not just one marker either, but about five, as other regiments were also there along with a battery from Iowa. The entire town of Vicksburg has hundreds if not thousands of signs, stone markers, and cannons where the troops had been.

Figure 50. Marker for the 46th Illinois in Vicksburg, Mississippi (author photo).

I knew Daniel survived the fighting at Vicksburg, but as I drove to the National Cemetery, it quickly became obvious that thousands did not. More Union soldiers are buried in Vicksburg National Cemetery than anywhere else in the United States, and the numbers are staggering: 17,000 Union soldiers, including 13,000 whose names were unknown. Included in these numbers were 7,000 Black soldiers, mostly in unknown graves. Soldiers' Rest is a small section designated for 5,000 Confederate soldiers, 3,500 of them marked as unknown. Grant was the first to arm and train former enslaved Black men who flocked to his camps. They fought gallantly at the Battle of Milliken's Bend, but the fatalities in their ranks were extremely high.

CHAPTER 14:

Camp Cowan, Hebron, Mississippi, November 1863– January 1864

Honor to the soldier and sailor everywhere, who bravely bears his country's cause. Honor, also, to the citizen who cares for his brother in the field and serves, as he best can, the same cause. — Abraham Lincoln

In the spring of 2018, I completed a particularly important part of my research at the Courthouse Museum in Vicksburg, Mississippi. For many years, I had this copy of Daniel's re-enlistment certificate. It is my most cherished document because it has his actual signature.

For many years I could not figure out where Camp Cowan at Hebron, Mississippi, was located. It was at that location that Daniel, as well as most of the other soldiers in the 46th, made the decision to re-enlist as veteran volunteers. He had been injured at Shiloh, had been sick numerous times, served faithfully for the two years of his initial enlistment, and could have gone home. However, he decided to stay with his regiment and re-enlisted, as did most of the remaining soldiers in the 46th. For their dedicated service, they each received a $100 bonus or bounty.

The day I stopped at the Courthouse Museum in Vicksburg, Mississippi, there were two men working in the archives room. One of the men was the man I previously mentioned, Gordon A. Cotton. Mr. Cotton was a true Southerner and was a teacher, author, and historian. I had my binder of information and told them what I was looking for. I showed them Daniel's enlistment document, and they started digging. These two wonderful historians found

CAMP COWAN, HEBRON, MISSISSIPPI, NOVEMBER 1863–JANUARY 1864

the answer and uncovered a fascinating part of Daniel's story. The soldiers were not camped at the present-day Hebron, Mississippi, but at a really fascinating plantation named LaGrange, owned in the 1860s by John Hebron and located about twenty miles east of Vicksburg on Clear Creek. Originally

Mr. Hebron raised cotton but changed over to planting fruit orchards that were very productive. Grant's army camped in this area for a long time since they had a good supply of food from the plantation. Even after the war ended, thousands of troops camped here to keep order and protect the freed Black people living there.

The regimental history notes:

> On the 28th of November we moved camp to Camp Cowan, near Clear Creek, nine miles from Vicksburg. Here the construction of comfortable log barracks was immediately commenced and soon completed, making it one of the most pleasant and comfortable camps it had ever been our good fortune to occupy.

(Jones)

RESIDENCE OF JOHN HEBRON, LaGrange Nursery
Warren County, Miss.

I spent a great deal of time driving around the area of Bovina and Clear Creek, and as I was driving down a back road, I spotted a beautiful home. On the gate was a sign that said LaGrange! It was part of the property that had once belonged to John Hebron and the area where Camp Cowan was located. I was able to find the telephone number for the owners and the next day had a wonderful conversation with them. I received an invitation to come back sometime and visit, and I also sent the owners a packet of all the historical documents that I had found at the courthouse. It was an exciting part of my research!

Figure 51. "Lagrange Plantation" (author photo).

CHAPTER 15:
Home to the Farm, January–February 1864

Don't try to stop me, don't stand in my way
I'm bound for the hills where the cool waters flow
On this road that will take me home.

— Mary Fahl

After re-enlisting, Daniel and the remaining 353 soldiers of the 46th Illinois received a furlough to return home to Northern Illinois in January of 1864 to recruit more soldiers to replace those who were injured or killed. They were also able to visit their loved ones back home. The winter of 1864 was cold and rainy in northern Mississippi, so the timing was good, and the soldiers were no doubt extremely excited to head home for a while. They left Camp Hebron on January 10, 1864, and stopped in Vicksburg where they formed in front of General McPherson's headquarters and saluted him. He in turn gave a speech praising them as being the first regiment to re-enlist as a veteran regiment in his department. Then the regimental history describes the scene as they left Mississippi:

> *The steamer Planet was at the wharf waiting to receive us, and upon which we embarked at once. On the afternoon and night of the 11th the men were all paid on muster out rolls and advance pay as veterans, by Maj. Stewart, paymaster. Early on the morning of the 12th our steamer pulled out and slowly passed up the river through heavy masses of floating ice, on account of which the boat had to tie up every night.*

(Jones)

Steamer Planet was a 600-ton stern-wheeler launched in 1856 at Cincinnati, Ohio. It was destroyed on February 1, 1864, when it was stranded and lost at College Point, Louisiana. The owner in 1856 was Henry E. Ealer, and the captain from 1856 until the Civil War was John Malloy. In 1861, the captain was J.T. Beurdeau. Until the Civil War, it was primarily a freight boat. After the Confederates surrendered at Port Hudson, it was used as a prison transport.

When the Steamer Planet arrived in Cairo, Illinois, on January 20, 1864, the soldiers transferred to trains on the Illinois Central Railroad to make the remaining journey through Illinois to Freeport arriving on January 23. Word had reached the citizens of Freeport that the 46th would be returning to Freeport by the end of January. Daniel's mother Olive, his brother John, and his sister Ellen would have heard the news as it was relayed from others, and preparations began for their homecoming. The citizens of Freeport quickly organized a banquet and celebration for their beloved soldiers. The following article in the Freeport Journal provides an incredibly detailed account of their homecoming:

ARRIVAL OF THE FORTY-SIXTH

The gallant Forty-Sixth Regiment Illinois Volunteers arrived in the city on Saturday last, and was met at the depot by an immense crowd of our citizens, eager to honor the brave men who had gone from among us to the battlefield. As the train came in the firing of cannon, the waving of flags, and the glad shouts of the thousands of men, women and children told the "boys" how strong a hold they had upon the affections and sympathies of the people. Accustomed as they are to discipline, it did not, however, in all cases restrain them, for as the boys rested upon the form of an aged father, a fond mother, a sister or brother, who stood trembling with emotion at the safe return of their loved one the stern soldier became the tenderhearted man, and eagerly sought the embrace of his friends. The regiment soon formed, and, preceded by a number of our most prominent citizens on horseback, and the Union Cornet Band, took up the line of march for Plymouth Hall. Many of the houses on Stephenson Street were decorated with flags, whose broad stripes and bright stars looked a joyous welcome to their brave defenders. Arrived in front of Plymouth Hall the regiment halted, and were formally welcomed by Col. T. J. Turner, on behalf of the citizens, in an exceedingly appropriate speech as follows:

Soldiers of the Gallant Forth-Sixth Regiment: The pleasing duty as been assigned to me, in behalf of the people of Stephenson County, to welcome you back to your friends and to our hospitalities; but when I look upon the scene before me, I feel the utter poverty of words to express that welcome. Here are your fathers and your mothers, your brothers and sisters, and here are all the people with throbbing hearts, and some with streaming eyes, impatient to seize you by the hands and clasp you to their hearts in the embrace of love and friendship, intensified by the sufferings and perils through which you have passed, and the glorious achievements you have won. Why this ovation? Why this spontaneous outpouring of the people of all ages? Why do these women and children, disregarding the snow and wet, press into the crowd to bid you welcome? It is because all of every age and condition desire to testify their gratitude and express their admiration of the brave men who periled everything for the honor of their country. You forsook your homes and all you held dear for the trials and dangers of the camp and battlefield, to preserve the life of the nation and the liberties of the people. How faithfully you have performed your duty, your thinned ranks most eloquently testify. You are not all here. Donelson and Shiloh, Metamora, and the inhospitable hills around Vicksburg all claimed their tribute; and the swamps and hospitals have witnessed their harvest of death. When grape and canister, the Minnie ball and bursting shell, poured down their iron hail, cutting down your commanders on every side, there you stood, with unbroken front, dealing death and destruction to the enemies of your country, and your shouts of victory have been heard on more than on battlefield. For these things we love you and honor you; but Oh! How that love is intensified, how our admiration swells up beyond the power of utterance, when we reflect that you have done so much; when you had nearly served out the full term of your enlistment, when you had performed your part so well; when you had done as that your country had ought to ask of you; when the joys and comforts of home and an honorable retirement invited you to return to the peaceful pursuits of life, you turned your back upon them all and re-entered the service of your country for another term. You had stood by our common mother through her darkest hours of trial, and you would not forsake her so long as a rebel foot profaned any portion of our country. By that crowning set of your loyalty and devotion you have set a noble example to other regiments, and made a most touching and eloquent appeal to the young men who have not yet born arms in defense of their country. Oh! That your appeal may be heeded, and when the short term of your adjourn amongst us is ended, may we behold your ranks filled to their maximum with patriots like yourselves.

I would speak of the glorious dead of your regiment, but the occasion is one of joy, and I will not sadden your hearts by bringing up before you the bright array of names and dwelling upon the deeds of those of your comrades in arms who gave their lives to their country. Their memory is enshrined deep in the hearts of all of us; their glowing deeds and their fame belong to our country and faithfully will she preserve the sacred trust.

We shall do all we can to make your stay amongst us pleasant, and when you take up your line of march again you will be flowed as you ever have been, by the prayers of Christian men and women, by their blessings and the good wishes of all.

Again, in behalf of this multitude here assembled—in behalf of the people

> *of Stephenson County—I bid you welcome.*
>
> *At the conclusion of Colonel Turner's remarks and while the soldiers were stacking arms, the band played the sweet air of "Home Again," after which, at the command of Colonel Turner, the boys "charged" upstairs, upon the good things which had been provided for their refreshment.*

The article goes on to explain how the plans were initially made for a basket lunch for each soldier when they returned. The time of their return was uncertain until Friday evening, and then the plans changed and "bills were sent out asking the citizens to prepare what they could for the dinner." At the conclusion of Colonel Turner's speech, Daniel and the other soldiers headed up the stairs to partake in a feast.

Our family does not have any diaries or letters that tell of Daniel returning to the farm, but no doubt John and even his mother and sister were in Freeport that cold January day to welcome him back and take their brother back home to the farm. In another small segment of the same page of the article is more about the food:

> *The dinner was excellent—roast beef, roast turkeys, geese, chickens, boiled hams, chicken pies, all hot, and cakes, pies, bread, etc, and excellent coffee. There was so much food that leftovers were sent to the camp of the regiment on the fairgrounds. Colonel Dornblaster also asked the soldiers to thank those who prepared the delicious food and called for three cheers for the ladies, which were given with a will, when the regiment retired from the Hall.*
>
> *The Freeport Journal pronounced:*
>
> *FURLOUGH—Most of the members of the Forty-Sixth have already left here on furlough for thirty days. All who desire will have that time allowed in which to visit their families and friends. At the completion of their furlough they will report to camp in this city. It is probable that for the next thirty days but few of the members of the regiment will be in camp here.*

For the month of February, Daniel was back home, in the same house where I grew up. It was not until I researched and found the article in the newspaper that I knew that Daniel had come back to the farm as a Civil War soldier. I lived in the old farmhouse briefly again in 2014 and thought often of Daniel being in the house with his mother, brother, and sister. How happy they must have been to spend this time together. He probably spent a lot of time talking about all of the places he had seen, as well as some of the horrible things that had happened during the battles. He no doubt went outside to help his brother John work on the farm, and they probably spent time down by the Pecatonica River. It was a time of joy for all of them, but also a time of sorrow as his time grew near to leave again. His dedication to his regiment must have been extraordinarily strong for him to leave his home, family, and the farm where he had spent his boyhood. But he did leave, returning at the end of his furlough to Freeport where he and the other soldiers of the 46th boarded the train once again to head back south. The recruitment of more soldiers was successful during the time home, and the regiment was now up to full strength with 987 enlistees.

CHAPTER 16:
Mississippi, March–July 1864

Once let the black man get upon his person the brass letters, U.S., let him get an eagle on his button, and a musket on his shoulder and bullets in his pocket, there is no power on earth or under the earth which can deny that he has earned the right of citizenship in the United States.
— Frederick Douglass, July 6, 1863

Daniel and the soldiers of the 46th Infantry returned to Camp Cowan at Hebron, Mississippi, at the beginning of March 1864. Since there were many new recruits, they vigorously drilled from March 10 until April 5, 1864. Then Brigadier General John McArthur led an expedition May 4–21, 1864. The objective of this expedition was to drive out remaining Confederate troops from Northern Mississippi. It was a significant expedition for Daniel, as it may have been the first time he fought with Black soldiers. The 3rd Colored Cavalry was part of the expedition, as shown on the chart on the next page. The 3rd USCT went on to become the famous "Buffalo Soldiers." Below is a recruitment poster used to recruit Black soldiers to fight for the Union.

Union Troops

Post of Vicksburg: Brigadier General John McArthur

- 1st Brigade: Colonel Benjamin Dornblaser
  - 46th Illinois Infantry
  - 76th Illinois Infantry

- 2nd Brigade: Lieutenant Colonel James H. Coates
  - 11th Illinois Infantry
  - 72nd Illinois Infantry
  - 124th Illinois Infantry
- Artillery: Captain Bolton
  - 2nd Illinois Light Artillery, Company C
  - 7th Ohio Battery

- Cavalry: Colonel Osband
  - 1st Kansas Mounted Infantry
  - 5th Illinois Cavalry
  - 11th Illinois Cavalry
  - 3rd USCT Cavalry

Confederate Troops

Department of Alabama, Mississippi, & East Louisiana: Lieutenant General Stephen D. Lee

- Wirt's Cavalry Brigade: Brigadier General W. Wirt Adams

Battles

- Benton, May 7–9, 1864
- Luce's Plantation, May 13, 1864
- Vaughn Station, May 15, 1864

During the Yazoo City Expedition, Daniel and the other soldiers marched hundreds of miles in the heat and dust of Mississippi. There were fierce short battles and constant skirmishes as they moved along roads near Benton, the Big Black River, the Illinois Central Railroad, Yazoo City, Vaughn's Station, and Lexington Road. The expedition report describes that the final skirmish took place near Vaughn's Station, where afterwards the troops camped for the night. The next day they started slowly moving back toward Vicksburg, traveling through Benton, Yazoo City, Liverpool, Satartia and finally to Haine's Bluff near Vicksburg, having marched close to two hundred miles.

George Oscar Cooper, another soldier in Company B of the 46th Illinois, marched these long miles with Daniel. George wrote the following account to his sister back home in Dixon, Illinois:

"We did not accomplish much on the expedition yet we did all that was expected of us-and probably more, even if we had not accomplished anything against the enemy, the benefits derived from the trip, in the improvement of health, are fully compensated as for our trouble- the boys returned in excellent health and spirits. There was enough of fighting to keep up the excitement and change the current of our thoughts from home recollection. Yet we are devoid of exciting news like you, our eyes are on Grant & Sherman. May victory perch upon their banners, and give us once more a peacefull happy & United country-we have northern dates up to the 6th so far we have reason to be gratefull, yet we are none the less anxious—for the great crisis is not past yet."

MISSISSIPPI, MARCH–JULY 1864

The 46th Illinois spent the remainder of May and the month of June in a camp near Vicksburg where Daniel and the other soldiers drilled, had picket duty, and performed camp duty. George wrote more about their time in camp:

*"...there is none of the hurry
and bustle of war—the guns which
one year ago sent death and
destruction
in our ranks—now awake us
from our slumbers at sunrise and
warn us of the approach of night-at
sunset. Our duties are quite light
in the meantime—having but very little
Guard duty to do—and scarcely
any drill thanks for the latter to
the rough conditions of the ground.
Our camp is situated on a hill
near the old "Father of Waters" health
Is excellent and the boys enjoy them
-selves as well as could be expected.
our camp presents a lively appear
-ance after dark. The ridges
around being illuminated by camp
fire & lights—while every variety
of music greets the ear."*

"The ridges around being illuminated by camp fires & lights—while every variety of music greets the ear." This line from George's letter beautifully describes the evening setting with the musicians entertaining the soldiers. Isaac Bolender, age 23, was one of the musicians for Company B. He had re-enlisted as a veteran volunteer along with Daniel the previous December. Isaac was from Rock Grove, Illinois, and survived the war, eventually settling in Iowa where he lived until his death at age 62 on April 22, 1904.

Daniel was marked present on the company muster rolls after he returned to Mississippi in March for the Yazoo City Expedition, and then for the Jackson Expedition. The Jackson Expedition included the 46th, the 76th, and the 8th Illinois infantry regiments and began on July 1, 1864. The soldiers fought more skirmishes on this expedition and also built a pontoon bridge over the Big Black River, similar to the one in this photo, for supply wagons to use.

They were involved in some fierce fighting on the Canton Road and held back the enemy for two hours until the Union supply train had passed. Then they returned to camp on July 9, 1864 "without further annoyance."

> *Thirty-six soldiers from the 46th regiment were captured during this expedition. The wounded of the command that fell into the hands of the enemy were very kindly treated, so much so that the wounded men spoke it of in the highest terms of praise and as soon as they were able, an amicable exchange of prisoners was appointed. The ceremony of exchange took place just outside the old fortifications of the city and was the occasion of much good feeling among the prisoners.*
>
> *(Jones)*

Prisoner exchanges like this one throughout the war did not always happen. Typically, officers might be exchanged while the other soldiers were sent to prison camps. I speculate that this exchange took place peacefully because General Grant was so generous with the terms of surrender at Vicksburg and paroled all of the Confederate soldiers at that time. Moreover, the "Yankees" were helping to rebuild war-torn Vicksburg, and the troops were helping to keep order during a challenging time for the city.

CHAPTER 17:
Morganza, Louisiana, July 29– August 30, 1864

Hope is like the sun, which, as we journey toward it, casts the shadow of our burden behind us. — Samuel Smiles

Daniel and the rest of the 46th Illinois and the 76th Illinois arrived at the Union camp at Morganza, Louisiana on July 29, 1864, after riding the steamer Adam from Vicksburg. They quickly built shades and arbors to survive the oppressive sun and heat. This camp was well known as one of the deadliest camps in the country. Disease was rampant, and the men suffered greatly from the heat, humidity, and mosquitoes. The 62nd, 65th, and 67th Colored Regiments were also camped at Morganza and were hit hard by disease, losing one-third of their soldiers, 1,374 of 3,158 men. Daniel and many other soldiers suffered during the summer of 1864 at Camp Morganza. Point Coupee historian Brian Costello describes the camp in his book A History of Pointe Coupee Parish:

> *Following the Union fiasco during the Red River Campaign, General Banks' Federal corps made camp at Morganza on May 22. They erected an earthen fort and a city of tents along the batture, just across the levee from the destroyed site of the village of Morganza. Many Federals died during that torrid summer and were buried on the Batture, whose site is now well within the bed of the Mississippi owing to its gradual westward shift.*

In 2018 and again in 2020, I drove to the Gulf Coast and spent time visiting more places in Louisiana and Mississippi where Daniel and the 46th were in the summer of 1864, including Morganza. One of my misguided beliefs for many years was that the members of the Lobdell family were all

Northerners, fought for the Union and never owned slaves. That could not be further from the truth! A few years before I visited the Gulf Coast for the first time, I worked on the genealogy of the Lobdell family and discovered a whole branch of our family had moved south in the early 1800s. They were sugar cane planters, owned slaves, and fought for the Confederacy! When Daniel and the 46th spent time at the Union Army camp at Morganza, Louisiana, he was close to some of his Lobdell cousins on plantations in the area.

Abraham and James Lobdell, my first cousins-six times removed, were born in the state of New York, but moved to the rich delta area at the end of the 1700s when the area was still owned by Spain and was known as West Florida. In 1803, Abraham bought land near present day Baton Rouge, Louisiana. He and other members of the Lobdell family were cotton and sugar cane planters, started many local businesses including a tavern, sawmill, and a drug store in an area that became known as Lobdell, Louisiana. Their plantation included a church and even a boarding school at one time. They never severed their ties with their family in New York, as some of the younger children were sent back there for school. Other members of the Lobdell family also moved to the South, where at the time large sums of money could be made, especially in the sugar cane business. In many of the Civil War era maps, "Lobdell Store" was labeled on maps and referred to in military reports, diaries, and letters.

A year before Daniel was at Morganza, there was a battle nearby at Stirling Plantation that also had ties to the Lobdell families in Louisiana. Anne Stirling was the daughter of Lewis Stirling who owned Stirling Plantation.

MORGANZA, LOUISIANA, JULY 29–AUGUST 30, 1864

Figure 52. The Lobdell Store in Lobdell, Louisiana.

She married John Little Lobdell, and together they owned Wakefield Plantation near St. Francisville across the Mississippi River from Morganza. The Confederates defeated the Union forces in this battle that took place on the Stirling Plantation, and they took many Union soldiers prisoner. The Union soldiers who escaped returned to Morganza and burned the town to the ground in retaliation. Morganza Landing on the Mississippi River was still there and being used, so the local people began rebuilding their town. The area remained an important spot on the Mississippi River, and Union soldiers continued to camp there as the fighting continued.

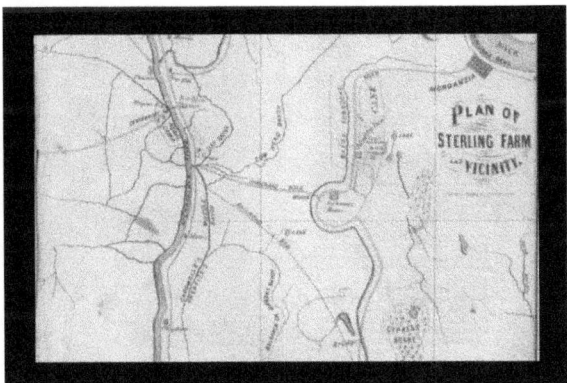

Figure 53. Map of the Battle of Stirling Plantation shows "Morganza" next to the Mississippi River

Although there are no records to show exactly where the camps were, with over 30,000 soldiers, the camps would have spread out for miles around Morganza Landing and all along the banks of the Mississippi River. In January of 2020, I decided to return to Morganza to complete more research and continue writing. I met with local historians and townspeople while I stayed at the RV park in town. They told me more about the history of the area, including an area called "Yankee Deadening." Local author Edwin Lyle Brown describes the area known as Yankee Deadening near Morganza:

> *Morganza was burned to the ground in 1863 and was only slowly being reoccupied. The Union forces were domiciled between the river and the levee with virtually no clear space for cemeteries. Soldiers were dying at the rate of at least one or two a day. The open and available space for burying this many people was obviously the space formerly occupied by buildings and so it was there that many bodies were buried. In recent years, bones have been dug up while excavating in the area. In many cases, they were simply pushed out of the site being dug and reinterred without ceremony nearby. As should be expected, there are numerous ghost stories about the spirits of fallen soldiers haunting houses in the town.*

Figure 54. Morganza Spillway at Sunset (author photo).

MORGANZA, LOUISIANA, JULY 29–AUGUST 30, 1864

There were mostly cotton plantations close to Morganza with the sugarcane plantations located farther south along the river. Some of the Northern soldiers wrote home about life in the South, including information about the enslaved. The following letter is interesting in its comparison of how Northerners viewed free Black people versus how this soldier described the lives of the enslaved he observed in the South. They had heard stories about life in the South. Now when they were there living with the local people, they could make observations for themselves like this soldier R.G. made in the summer of 1864:

FROM THE 175TH BATTALLION N. Y. V.—

The following interesting letter from a former Trojan reached us yesterday:

MORGANZIA, La., June 15, 1864.

Editor Whig—Sir: Movements of such great magnitude occurring in Virginia may so eclipse our movements here that any information I may send you will be skipped over as unworthy of a passing glance, and, perhaps with justice, as there is certainly nothing transpiring that will compare, in the remotest degree with the unparalleled [sic] events which are now reddening the soil of the Old Dominion with blood. But, while I am fortunately unable to depict great battles causing immense human sacrifices, there is left to me the more pleasing task of penning a few sentences on southern life and manners.

It may be thought by many persons of the North that the negro is treated by the white population of the South as a being little superior to the brute; but experience has taught me that quite the reverse is the fact. This erroneous idea, no doubt, arises from a consideration of the abject condition of the slave, which supposes him to be shut out from all commingling and association with the whites. Now in contrasting them in this respect with the colored population of the North I find that, while at the North the prejudice against them is so intense that white persons will not associate with them in the street, in the Church, nor dwell with them in the same house, here at the South they do all these, and, in addition, publicly live together as man and wife, raising in many instances large families, without occasioning any remarks from their neighbors. The negro maid is the young southern lady's confidante in matters of love, and any person who may wish to take the trouble can see in the large towns the mistress and servant sitting side by side in the same carriage engaged in familiar and agreeable conversation, without any display of pompous dignity on the part of the Southern lady. To be sure morality stands not so high as with the rigid puritan spirit of the North, nor is the condition of marriage thought so sacred; but still there is less of that degraded licentiousness which we meet in every street and at every turn of our northern cities. In consequence of the above intermingling of the whites and blacks, persons are to be met with here of every shade of color, making it in some instances difficult to determine where the Negro ends or the white begins. Northern miscegenationists have a practical illustration of their system here, at least in the towns, the Negroes on plantations being generally purely African.

Frankness and affability are prominent traits of the southern character, and a few gentlemanly, spoken words is enough to make a southerner your friend, which friendship he denotes with an ardor of expression unknown to more sterile climes.—Hospitality too is exercised to that degree that I have known it to be extended to enemies, as in the case of our "drummer boys " who, straggling behind, were on more than one occasion kindly brought into the houses on the road-side by the inmates who, beholding their youth kindly caressed them, pitying their condition and loading their haversacks with, to them, rare delicacies.

I do not know but my remarks will be construed by your readers into "sympathy for the South," and that I will be called "Copperhead" or some other such unmeaning name, but truth compels me to state facts as I find them, and however much I may condemn the act of secession, I may surely be permitted to give the result of my observations.

The women here are generally very independent and as regards the "rebellion" quite out-spoken. They do not conceal their aversion to Yankees, nor despair of the final triumph of Dixie; yet they are courteous, *affable and polite, but steadfast in their opinions, even though in some instances they depend on our army for support. They generally keep within doors, and are seldom seen promenading the streets of the towns, and seem to avoid, as much as possible, coming in contact with soldiers. (civilwarlouisiana.com)*

Figure 55. A sketch of the Union camps at Morganza from the collection of Mayor S.J. Tuminello, Morganza, Louisiana.

CHAPTER 18:
Daniel's Final March, August 1864

Where the battle rages, there the loyalty of the soldier is proved.
— *Martin Luther*

During the summer of 1864, Daniel and the Union Army were still camped at Morganza, Louisiana. Skirmishes continued with Confederate soldiers who were located to the west near the Atchafalaya River, which runs parallel to the Mississippi River in Southwest Louisiana. On August 8th, Colonel Jones and two hundred soldiers of the 46th went out on a scouting expedition and captured twelve Confederate soldiers, taking them as prisoners back to the Union camp in Morganza the next morning. The regimental history also describes the reorganization of the Brigade that took place that summer.

> *On the 13th of August, General Canby's order No. 93 was promulgated, assigning the regiment to the 1st Brigade, 2d Division, 19th Army Corps. The brigade to consist of the 8th, 11th, 46th and 76th Regiments of Illinois Infantry, and the 7th and 30th Missouri Infantry, and to be commanded by Col. B. Dornblaser, of the 46th Illinois Infantry, General Dennis to command the Division, and General Reynolds the Corps.*

(Jones 8446)

Throughout the Civil War, Daniel, like all soldiers, marched endless miles all over the South. At times, they boarded trains or steamboats for transport, but the majority of the time they marched from place to place. On August 23, 1864, the Brigade prepared to march on what was to be Daniel's final expedition. The destination was Clinton, Louisiana, a Confederate cavalry stronghold.

The town also had supplied food and ammunition to the Confederate Army and was on the Clinton rail line that had been destroyed earlier in the war. The objective was to drive the remaining Confederates from the area as the Union Army prepared for its march to Mobile, Alabama.

A primary document that I read while researching information about Morganza was the diary of Simon M. Bott, private in the 120th Infantry regiment of Ohio (E Company). Private Bott was also at the Union camp in Morganza and recorded events in his diary each day. In most of the entries he described the weather, noted if they drilled, and recorded that he was sick most of the time. Then on August 23, 1864, he wrote the following entry that noted his regiment left at 11:00 P.M.

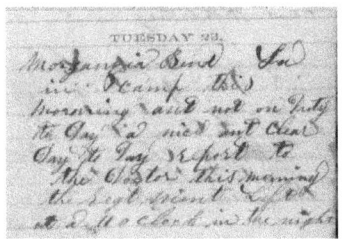

*Morganzia Bend, La (Louisiana)
in camp this morning and not on Duty
to Day a nice and clear
Day to Day report to
the Doctor this morning
the Regiment left at 11 o'clock in the night.*

Late in the evening of August 23, 1864, three thousand soldiers from the brigade boarded steamers and traveled south on the river to Port Hudson where they disembarked at Springfield Landing. The map on the following page shows Port Hudson and farther south on the west side of the river, the Lobdell Stores and the plantation of Daniel's distant cousin, John Little Lobdell. In 2020, I drove from Morganza, Louisiana, to Clinton, Louisiana, and on the drive, I thought about Daniel and the other soldiers marching all night to get there. It was not a short drive, so the march was probably very difficult, as there were swamps, creeks, rolling hills, and railroad tracks, not to mention Confederate soldiers nearby ready to shoot at the oncoming men. I stopped in Clinton to take some photos of this beautiful courthouse, built in 1840, so it was there when Daniel was in Clinton!

Colonel Dornblaser of the 46th Illinois authored the following report of the expedition that was one of six reports under the heading: "August 23–29, 1864—Expedition to Clinton, Louisiana with skirmishes (25th) at Olive Branch and the Comite River" in the official records of the war. The infantry

IN THE FOOTSTEPS OF DANIEL LOBDELL

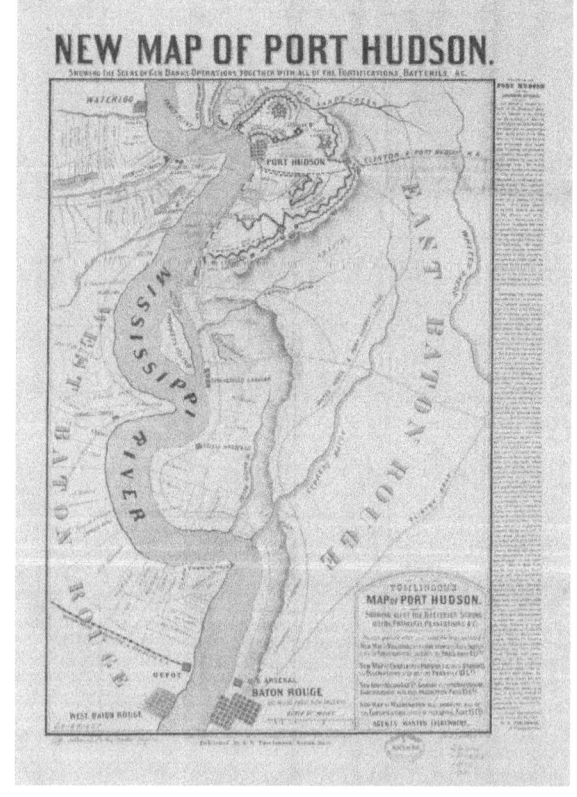

saw little action as this assault was mainly between Union and Confederate cavalry. There was a great deal of skirmishing, and the Confederate cavalry stronghold at Clinton was forced from its position. The Union brigade then simply returned to Morganza.

When the men returned, they were exhausted from marching so many miles.

>Headquarters 1st Brig. 2d Div., 19th A. C.
>
>Morganza, La., August 29th, 1864.
>
>CAPTAIN W. E. KUHN,
>
>*A. A. A. Gen. 2nd Div., 19th Army Corps.*
>
>*Captain:*—I have the honor to report that in compliance with orders, this Brigade embarked on steamers on the night of the 23d inst., and proceeded to Port Hudson, La., where it disembarked. On the evening of the 24th inst., at five o'clock P. M., the column moved out in the direction of Clinton, La., the 1st Brigade in advance, supplied with five days' rations and one ammunition wagon to each regiment. The command marched all night, only resting at intervals to enable the column to close up, and arrived at Clinton at noon of the 25th. Small scouting parties of the enemy only were encountered, who fled at our approach.
>
>The troops rested until four o'clock P. M. of the 26th, when the return march was commenced, arriving at Port Hudson on the morning of the 28th, and Morganza on the morning of the 29th.
>
>Port Hudson is distant twenty-five miles from here, and from Port Hudson to Clinton the same. The march was a very hard one and the losses sustained by the Brigade were caused principally by men becoming exhausted by the way and being captured by the enemy, who followed in our rear. The following are the losses of the Brigade: 11th Illinois, three missing; 46th Illinois, two missing; 76th Illinois, one missing; 30th Missouri, two missing.
>
>Respectfully your Obed't Serv't,
>
>B. DORNBLASER,
>
>Colonel Commanding Brigade.

It was August in Louisiana, and the heat was unbearable. On August 30, 1864, Daniel was admitted to the regimental hospital as is shown on his muster roll card. His complaint was acute diarrhea that was extremely common among the soldiers due to the unsanitary conditions in which they lived. Food and water were commonly contaminated with the bacteria Shigella and Salmonella. These hidden pathogens destroyed soldiers' intestinal systems, leading to pain, dehydration, and shock. Very little was available to help since antibiotics would not be discovered until 1928. Opium or whiskey was used for pain and quinine for illnesses such as malaria and dysentery, but these did nothing to stop bacterial infections. After surviving such a long, hot, brutal expedition, Daniel succumbed to his illness. He spent six days at the Regimental Hospital in camp and then on September 4, 1864, was sent to New Orleans to the General Hospital. Daniel would never again see his comrades of his beloved 46th Illinois.

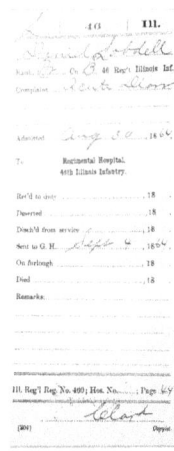

Figure 56. Olive Branch, Louisiana, area of the last skirmish for Daniel.

CHAPTER 19:
Barracks, U.S. General Hospital, New Orleans, August 30–September 19, 1864

The darkness takes him over, the sickness pulls him in. — Lang Leav

Daniel was taken to New Orleans on a hospital transport ship and admitted to the General Hospital at New Orleans Barracks. The hospital was built after the Mexican American War and was used extensively during the Civil War. The Union Army had captured New Orleans, one of the wealthiest cities in the country at the time, early in the war on May 1, 1862. The city was spared the destruction that so many other Southern cities suffered. Daniel's roll card shows that he was admitted on September 5, 1864, probably with hopes that he would recover and be able to rejoin his regiment. However, all treatment must have failed, and he was no doubt too weak to return to battle, so he was furloughed to go home on September 19, 1864.

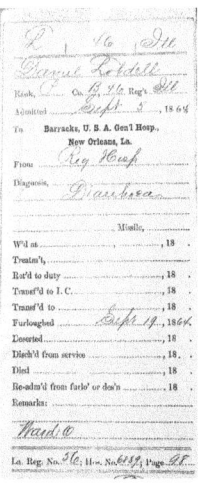

In 2005, Hurricane Katrina hit the Gulf Coast and as a result of the break in the levees, many areas of New Orleans, including Jackson Barracks saw catastrophic flooding. The day I visited Jackson Barracks to find information, it was sunny and warm. A small museum housed nice displays of the history of the barracks and the curator helped me find photos of what the barracks looked like during the Civil War. It was there that Daniel spent two weeks

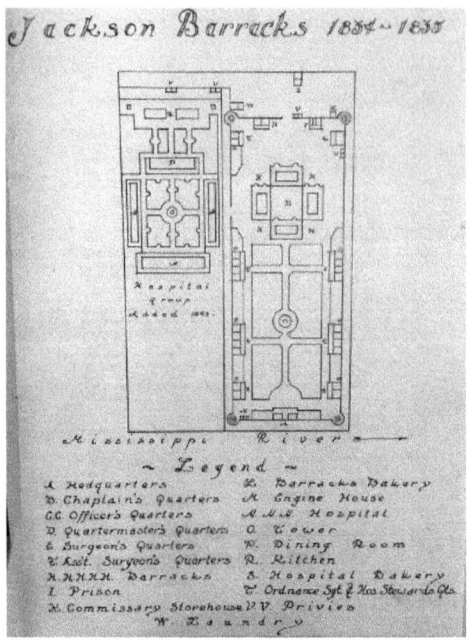

New Orleans and the U.S. Barracks saw increased military activity during the Mexican War (1846-1848). Adjacent land was purchased west of the original garrison and a U.S. Army hospital was constructed to treat sick and wounded soldiers. Construction was not completed until the conflict was over, but the hospital was used extensively during the U.S. Civil War in the 1860s.

trying to recover. Above is a drawing of the barracks that I obtained while visiting the complex in 2018.

I think it is important to include some information about the chaplain of the 46th Illinois, as I believe that Daniel's Christian faith was an important part of his life. Chaplains were especially important for the spiritual life of the soldiers, both while they were healthy and when they were sick. Hezekiah Lewis was the chaplain for the 46th Illinois Infantry throughout the war. Reverend Lewis, a Presbyterian minister, was born in 1821, so he was forty years old when he became the regimental chaplain. He was also married with three children when he joined the 46th Illinois. After the war, he continued his ministry and lived until 1914, passing away in Kansas at the age of ninety-three (Ancestry.com). Reverend Lewis probably met with Daniel while he was ill to pray for him and provide emotional support.

Description of the role of the chaplain in the war

COMRADE SPOFFORD

responded to the toast, "Chaplains of the War." He said that no class of men in the army were respected more than the chaplains. They were not always at the front during battle but they were always at the bedside of the sick and dying, administering to their spiritual wants, brightening up some poor dying soldier's pathway to that better land, or speaking words of encouragement to a homesick boy. He said when the boys wanted to ask their Heavenly Father to guide and protect them they always went to the Chaplain and asked through him as they were of the opinion that the Chaplain was better acquainted with the Lord. The Chaplains of the army did good service during the war, and their work should never be forgotten. Their work did not cease with the war—for the past twenty-five years they have been leading the boys through the perils of civil life to that Grand Master of Comrades in that life beyond.

CHAPTER 20:
Mound City Hospital, Cairo, Illinois, September–October 1864

Those who have long enjoyed such privileges as we, forget in time that men have died to win them. — Franklin D. Roosevelt

Daniel was transported on a hospital ship from Jackson Barracks in New Orleans to the U.S.A. Post Hospital at Mound City, Illinois. This hospital was located near Cairo, Illinois, and Daniel was admitted on September 29, 1864. There are no final records or reports about Daniel's last days. By that time, he might have been unconscious from malnourishment and dehydration due to chronic diarrhea. The historic photo below depicts the scene of how Daniel would have been moved from a hospital ship into the hospital.

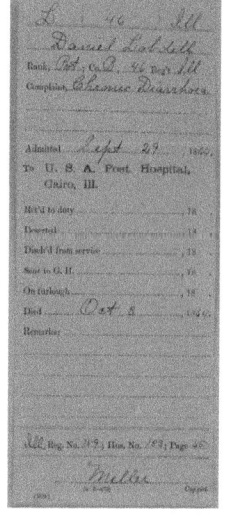

Courtsey of: Congregation of the Sisters of the Holy Cross, St. Mary's Notre Dame

The U.S. General Hospital at Mound City was a part of the Cairo complex of Army and Navy facilities at the confluence of the Ohio and the Mississippi Rivers. The USN Red Rover hospital ship often docked there. Free Black women and also Nuns (Sisters of the Holy Cross of Saint Mary's Convent from South Bend, Indiana) staffed the hospital. It became the operational base for staffing Red Rover and eight

MOUND CITY HOSPITAL, CAIRO, ILLINOIS, SEPTEMBER–OCTOBER 1864

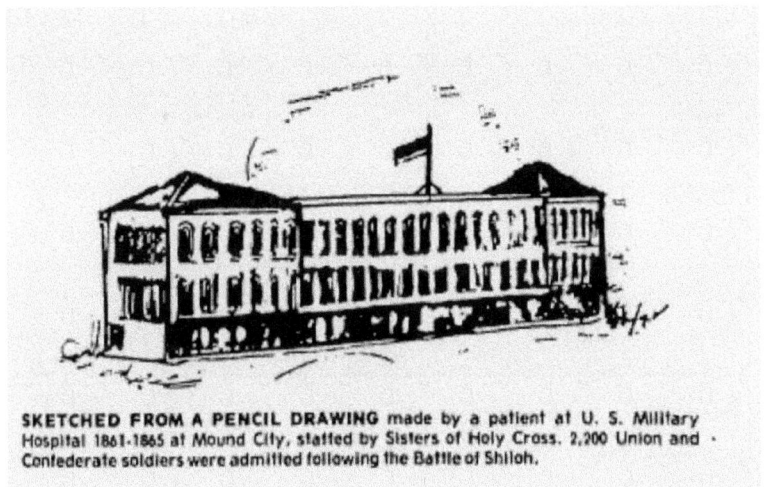

SKETCHED FROM A PENCIL DRAWING made by a patient at U. S. Military Hospital 1861-1865 at Mound City, staffed by Sisters of Holy Cross. 2,200 Union and Confederate soldiers were admitted following the Battle of Shiloh.

shore hospitals of the West. The hospital's main building, in the sketch above, was a converted warehouse. Dr. Horace Warnder was surgeon-in-charge. The women were not accepted right away, but because of their excellent work getting the hospital clean and orderly, as well as the excellent care they gave to patients, the men in charge soon changed their minds.

In a letter to his mother in December 1861, Father Neal Gillespie wrote:

General Wallace and the officers of the Brigade, who are all men of education and high standing and considerable influence at home, are delighted with the Sisters and at the great good they are doing in the hospitals in Paducah. There is a chaplain for each of the three regiments, one a Methodist, the other a Presbyterian, of whom M. Angela speaks as being very worthy men, and another of some other denomination ... the surgeons there, as well as those connected with the Mound City Hospital, seven or eight in number, the stewards and the soldier-nurses are also much pleased with the way things go since the arrival of the Sisters; although there was great opposition there, as in Cairo, to their coming.

The conditions at most hospitals were deplorable. At Mound City, Mother Angela set forth reorganizing the wards. She assigned each sister to her post and duties and through the sisters' organization the floors were scrubbed clean of blood, bed linens were changed and the sick were bathed and served appetizing meals. The daily menu had been soggy bread and rancid pork, but Mother Angela changed all that. She requisitioned rice, eggs, milk and chickens from the quartermaster's stores and she prepared the food herself.

(Intravartalo)

During one of my first visits to Cairo, I searched for the site of the hospital. There is a marker pictured below. As I was looking at it, I spotted the grain bins and brick building across the street. I drove over, and a man was walking out. When I explained what I was searching for, he told me that the small brick portion was the only part left from the hospital, and the workers used part of it for a break room. Then I was thrilled when he asked if I would like to go in and look around! It was amazing to see the old beams and sense the history that took place there, as well as heartbreaking to know that Daniel spent his last days there so far from his home and family.

Figure 57. Historical marker for the Mound City Hospital (author photo)

MOUND CITY HOSPITAL, CAIRO, ILLINOIS, SEPTEMBER–OCTOBER 1864

Figure 58. The remaining brick structure of Mound City Hospital.

On October 3, 1864, Daniel died. The Sisters would have prepared his body for burial in the nearby cemetery, and a telegram was most likely sent to his mother Olive and brother John. At some point, the decision was made to have his body sent home to Northern Illinois from Cairo. My cousin Ron Holmes told me many years ago that John "went to get Daniel" after he died. That was the only bit of information that I have ever heard from my family about Daniel. It was unusual for a soldier's body to be sent back home when he died, but my Great-great grandfather John Lobdell pictured here, must have sent money to have Daniel's body embalmed, placed in a coffin, and sent back home by train to Freeport.

Figure 59. Daniel's older brother, John Lobdell, my great-great grandfather.

According to Dr. Gordan Dammann, Civil War Medical historian from Lena, Illinois, the regulations of the railroad at the time required that a body must be embalmed before being shipped home. Friends or possibly the chaplain could have also escorted his body home. This part I do not know, but I do know that John went somewhere with his team of horses hitched onto a wagon and brought his brother back home to the farm.

Daniel was twenty-three years old when he died, and his brother John was twenty-seven. John was not married in 1864 and was living on the farm with his mother Olive and sister Ellen who had just married Walter Ross on July 4, 1864. When news was sent that Daniel had died, his mother, brother, and sister must have been devastated.

In the mid-19th century, people in the north were primarily Christian and Protestant, and there was a belief in a "good" death...that one should die peacefully, surrounded by their family. Daniel's mother was no doubt distraught to learn that her youngest child had died in a hospital so far from their home and from the farm he loved. The process of mourning the dead was also important to families, and when John went to bring his brother home, that act of going to get him must have given comfort to their grief-stricken mother and sister.

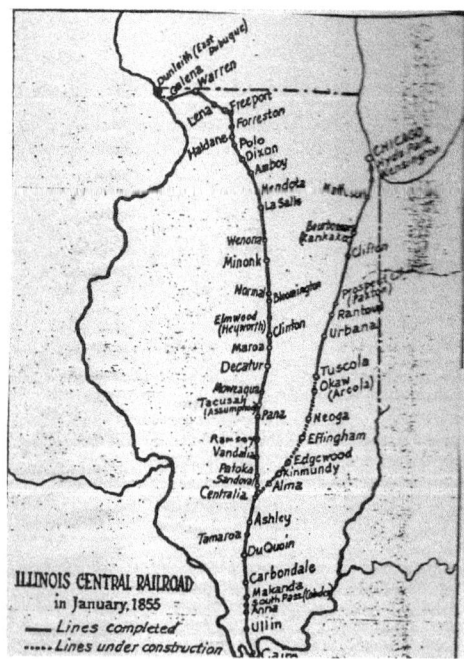

Figure 60. Map of the railroads in Illinois 1855.

CHAPTER 21:
Greenwood Cemetery, November 1864

"On thy grave the rain shall fall from the eyes of a mighty nation!"
— Thomas William Parsons

Greenwood Cemetery is located just a few miles from our farm, and I have traveled past it for over sixty years. It is here where my parents were both laid to rest in 2021. It was here that I first saw Daniel's tombstone and became interested in who this person was in our family history. Many years have now passed since I first started my research, and I feel that I have honored him by telling his story. He is no longer just a name on a tombstone but someone that withstood unbearable hardship and gave his life for our country. The very first document I ever found was Daniel's obituary that was printed in the Freeport Weekly Journal on November 23, 1864. It was preserved on microfilm at the local history room in the Freeport Public Library. I can only speculate what happened from the time Daniel died in Cairo on October 3 until his funeral, burial, and the publication of his obituary. The original copy on the next page was very difficult to read. It was clearer on the microfilm, and I was able to transcribe it. It gave me the first clues to his military service and inspired me to continue researching his life. His obituary was written by "P.V.H." The language was typical of the writing of the mid 19th century focusing on his patriotism, sacrifice, and strength of character.

Fallen Asleep

Died, in the hospital at Cairo, aged 23 years, Daniel Lobdell of Co. B, 46th Reg. IL. Vet Vols.

He joined the 46th when it was first mustered late service under the brave and lamented Col. Davis with that heroic band, he lay under the frowning guns of Donelson and Vicksburg. And fought on the bloody fields of Shiloh and Hatchie. At Shiloh he was wounded and received a furlough to visit his home in Waddams. After the battle of Hatchie, he fell into decline and his life was despaired of. Nobly retained a discharge which was tendered him, through sickness and suffering, and even the near approach of death, he followed the fortunes of his beloved regiment. He recovered his health and re-enlisted as a veteran volunteer. He participated in the marches and fighting of the second week of July in Alabama. Soon after he was again attacked by disease and went down to the grave. His friends brought home the dear dead form and laid it with their "loved and lost."

He was a generous, self-sacrificing, affectionate son and brother; as such his memory will live in the hearts of his friends as the verdure of spring, as the breath of summer from the fields of new mown hay. He was a brave soldier; as such he will be mourned by his comrades in arms. He was a true patriot; as such the friends of Freedom will lament him as they lament each and all of her fallen sons. He was, we trust, a Christian; though his body lay lo in the grave he shall yet come forth more lovely than the flowers of the field, more glorious than the stars of heaven.

Damascus, Ill. Nov. 20th
P.V.H.

Freeport Weekly Journal
23 November 1864
pg. 3 col. 5

Epilogue

After Daniel was sent home, the soldiers of the 46th Illinois moved from Morganza, Louisiana, to a camp on the banks of the Mississippi at what is now Kenner, Louisiana. I spent a few weeks camping at the KOA in Kenner and often walked along the levee of the river. Later, they moved to Dauphin Island, Alabama, another place where I camped for ten days. There they were part of the final battles to secure Mobile, Alabama. They were camped on the western side of Mobile when on April 16, 1865, the received great news:

> ...the glorious tidings of Lee's surrender to General Grant were confirmed and greeted with shouts of joy as the forerunner of the speedy overthrow of the entire rebellion. But the echoing sounds of exultation had not yet died away, when on the 20th the horrible news of the assassination of President Lincoln burst upon us like a clap of thunder from a clear sky, causing our rejoicing to be turned to bitter grief.
>
> (Woodbury)

After the surrender, they stayed in various places in Louisiana until their final furlough in December of 1865. The soldiers of the 46th were mustered out on January 20, 1866, and returned home.

In January 2020, I camped in Morganza, Louisiana (the final place Daniel camped) for a month to finish this book. The people I have met through the years have been so helpful and interesting. The battlefields and sites were beautiful, although it was heartbreaking thinking about what happened there. I always would think about how homesick Daniel must have been for the farm. It was during my research that I learned that he was able to go back home for a month the winter before he died. When I walked through the old farmhouse, it was incredible to think that he had been there too, as a soldier, spending time with his mother and brother. Many years ago, Daniel was just a name on a tombstone, but now he has a story. I hope to have honored his memory by telling his story.

APPENDIX A:
Daniel's Family

John Lobdell, Daniel's brother and my great-great grandfather. In 1865, Daniel's brother, John married Anna Foreman, and they had one son, William. John and Anna farmed the Lobdell homestead until 1895 when William took over.

PIONEER RESIDENT PASSED AWAY MONDAY MORNING

John Lobdell, one of Lena's prominent residents who has been very ill for the past 10 days, passed away Monday forenoon at the age of 86 years, 3 months and 11 days. The deceased was well known in Lena. He was born February 10, 1837, in Will county, Ill. When a child, 8 months old his parents moved to Stephenson county, settling on what is now the Lobdell homestead in Waddams township. Here he grew to manhood and on August 17, 1855, he was united in marriage to Miss Anna Foreman, of Lena, and they took up housekeeping on the homestead. To this union one son, William, was born. They remained on the farm until about 28 years ago when they moved to Lena where they had since resided with the exception of a few years when Mr. Lobdell moved back to the farm to make his home with his son after the death of his wife. He was a man of sterling qualities in the community in which he lived, a good neighbor, a true friend, helping those in need. His word was his bond, and a living example of true patriotic manhood. Surviving him are: his son, William

(Lena Weekly Star, May 24, 1923)

William Lobdell (front row, second from the left) was John and Anna Lobdell's only child. He was my Great grandfather and Daniel's nephew. He, his wife Emma Lobdell, and all their children lived at the farm. My Grandfather John F. Lobdell is in the back row, second from the right.

John Lobdell, my grandfather, married Leta Kappenman, and together they also farmed the same land and lived in the same house as Daniel from 1921-1954. They had four sons, Allen, Vernon, Robert, and my dad Mervin (the youngest).

APPENDIX A: DANIEL'S FAMILY

Lobdell Homestead. The farmhouse where Daniel grew up. The front part of the house was added in 1901.

Mervin John Lobdell, my father, married Verla Liebergesell. Together they also farmed the same land and lived in the same house as Daniel starting in 1954. They had four children, Murry, Kayla (Me), Karlyn, and Kelly.

Our family in 2001

Kayla F. Lobdell. I was born on May 13, 1960, and lived on the farm until 1983. I returned to the old farmhouse to live for a brief time in 2012, at which time I began my journey to finish tracing the history of my great-great granduncle Daniel Lobdell.

Stephenson County Civil War Memorial Monument in Freeport, Illinois. Daniel's name is on the north side of the monument.

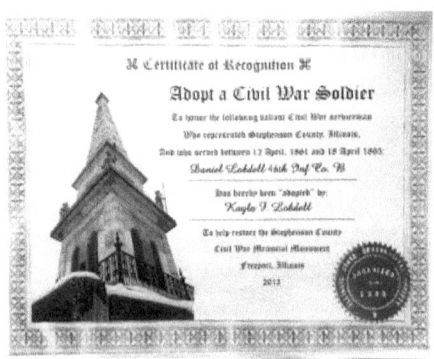

APPENDIX B:
Battlefields and Civil War-Related Sites

I visited all of these places during my research:
- Lobdell Farmhouse, near Lena, Illinois
- Lincoln Douglas Debate Site, Freeport, Illinois
- Camp Scott Site, Freeport, Illinois
- Camp Butler near Springfield, Illinois
- Cairo, Illinois
- Fort Donelson, Tennessee
- Fort Henry, Tennessee
- Shiloh Battlefield, Tennessee
- Corinth, Mississippi
- Memphis, Tennessee
- Bolivar, Tennessee
- Hatchie (Battle of Davis Bridge Battlefield Site), Tennessee
- Holly Springs, Mississippi
- LaGrange, Tennessee
- Vicksburg, Mississippi
- Camp Cowan, Hebron Plantation, Mississippi
- Plymouth Hall, Freeport, Illinois
- Yazoo City, Mississippi
- Jackson, Mississippi
- Morganza, Louisiana
- Port Hudson, Louisiana
- Clinton, Louisiana
- Olive Branch, Louisiana
- Jackson Barracks, New Orleans, Louisiana
- Mound City Hospital near Cairo, Illinois
- Greenwood Cemetery near Lena, Illinois

APPENDIX C:
Historians and Editors

Michael Bub I joined several Civil War pages on Facebook and it was on a post on one of these pages that I started chatting with Mike. I needed a lot of help and direction, and he was very helpful with my initial questions. Later, he helped me on several parts of this book, and in April 2024, he read through the whole book for a last final edit. He has become a great friend, and I appreciate all of the help that he has given me through the years. He was kind enough to write a short biography:

Michael Bub was born in St. Louis, Missouri, in 1965. He discovered at a young age he had a unique and curious passion for learning, especially about American military history. After graduation from Sikeston High School, he attended Southeast Missouri State University in Cape Girardeau and Tribeca University in Nashville, Tennessee, studying history and US military history, earning his master of arts degree. His resume in this field includes an appointment as director of education for the Tennessee Civil War Museum as well as a future with the National Park Service working at historic battlefields such as Chickamauga-Chattanooga, Shiloh, and Vicksburg National Military Parks. He also worked on various films such as Gettysburg and Andersonville among others, along with countless historical documentaries. Although valued in front of the camera, Bub also worked behind the scenes as a historical consultant and production assistant. His experience with publishing first came with a research position at Time-Life Books. He began writing independent articles for various Civil War publications and then in 1997 became a published author with his book A Thousand of Her Noblest Egyptians—a regimental history of the 81st Illinois Volunteer Infantry. From his early youth until more recent years, he has managed to stay anchored in the music industry as a musician, songwriter, and producer. Employment

APPENDIX C: HISTORIANS AND EDITORS

at Muscle Shoals Sound in Sheffield, Alabama, provided him the vehicle he needed to polish his production and engineering skills.

Gordon A. Cotton I met Mr. Cotton when I went to the Courthouse Museum in Vicksburg. He was really interested in the information that I had already collected, and he and another docent were extremely helpful in figuring out where Hebron Plantation was located east of Vicksburg. Sadly, he passed away in 2021. This article from the Vicksburg Post describes the wonderful man I met that day in Vicksburg, Mississippi, who told me that Vicksburg was pro-Union until they started shooting at us!

Gordon Cotton, a Vicksburg and Warren County icon who spent a lifetime learning and sharing history, himself made history in the way in which he did it. He was a man steeped in Southern heritage, educated in history and eloquent in his ability to share it, both in person and in the written word. He was cherished, beloved, respected and now, missed. Cotton died Sunday at the age of 84. "Among everything, he was a teacher," said Karen Gamble, former editor of The Vicksburg Post, but more importantly, a life-long friend of Cotton. "I spent an hour on the phone with him Friday. He was so upbeat, excited. We were discussing the plans for his fifth 80th birthday." Cotton would have marked his 85th birthday on April 4. Cotton was born in 1937 and raised in Campbell Swamp at Yokena in southeastern Warren County. He earned a bachelor's and master's degree from Mississippi College and taught at Jett, Redwood and Warren Central High School, as well as at was then Holmes Junior College. In addition to his dynamic historical works that lined the pages of The Vicksburg Post for years, Cotton was the author of more than 17 books detailing local and regional state history. "This morning," Dee Hyland said Sunday after learning of her friend's death, "I feel — knowing Gordon was a very strong Christian helps, but I am feeling sorry for myself because I will miss him so. He was a dear, dear friend and I loved him dearly." Cotton long served as director of the Old Court House Museum, and was described by friends as a "walking encyclopedia." But it is not the stories he could share that will be missed, it will be the gregarious soul that lived and shined within. "I've known Gordon since I was in high school and of course he is one of the most widely known and respected people in town and really all over the South with his historical connections and the work he had done at the newspaper with his (weekly Vicksburg Post) column," former publisher of The Vicksburg Post Pat Cashman said. "He was loved by so many people around this area and so knowledgeable — the books he has written, he is just an encyclopedia of knowledge of all the history here. He was sort of the walking textbook — he knew everything about the people here." Bubba Bolm, director of the Old Court House Museum, who worked with Cotton and later succeeded him, said "Gordon's passing is a huge, huge loss for our city, state and beyond. We will miss him greatly. He was a great historian, teacher, and a friend whose stories about our community will continue to live on." "He was a walking encyclopedia of everything that was Vicksburg and Warren County," Hyland said. "As one of my very closest friends, I will miss him terribly." Cotton's friend Kelle Barfield, who owns Lorelei Books downtown and serves as District 5 Supervisor, said she will always remember him fondly. "We will remember Gordon as a prolific writer and historian. But as much as he stands apart as one of the greatest storytellers Warren County will ever know, Gordon sets an example to each of us of the power of our story and of our connection to one another," Barfield said. "He encouraged me to start doing some writing of my own and was overjoyed when my son A.D. sought his help with genealogical research. Gordon leaves a legacy of books and writings that tell our collective history as well as a challenge to keep recording and sharing our personal chapters in the ongoing story of our community life. "I already miss him dearly, but Gordon will never be fully gone as long as we keep the stories alive," Barfield continued. Cotton was a member and deacon of Shiloh Primitive Baptist Church and also attended Yokena Presbyterian Church. He was a member of the First Families of Mississippi, the Vicksburg and Warren County Historical Society, the Mississippi Historical Society and the Sons of Confederate Veterans. In 2005, Cotton was honored with the First Families of Mississippi's award for leadership in genealogy and historic preservation. Cotton received the award of Meritorious Leadership in Mississippi History,

APPENDIX C: HISTORIANS AND EDITORS

Genealogy and Historic Preservation from the Order of the First Families of Mississippi, a state historic-preservation group for descendants of people who lived in what is now Mississippi from 1699 until it became a state in 1817. Helen Yates Price, in a letter nominating Cotton for the award in 2004, said he "is an internationally known author and a much-sought-after source of Southern, Mississippi and Vicksburg history." Funeral services for Cotton were held Tuesday at Glenwood Funeral Home with burial at Jordan's Chapel Cemetery on Campbell Swamp Road — near the church built by Cotton and his friend, Hobbs Freeman. Post writers Tim Reeves, Terri Cowart Frazier and John Surratt contributed to this report.

Lyle Brown I met Lyle and his wonderful wife, Pam when I camped at Morganza, Louisiana, for two months. They lovingly called me Morganza's first "Snowbird!" Lyle was full of information about Morganza and the "Yankees," including Daniel, who once camped there.

Brian James Costello I met Brian when I went to the Point Coupee Library, and he was helpful in finding some books for me to use in my research of Morganza.

Brian was born in 1966 and is an American historian, author, archivist, and humanitarian. He is an 11th generation resident of New Roads, Louisiana, seat of Pointe Coupee Parish. He is three-quarters French and one-quarter Italian in ancestry.

He graduated from False River Academy in New Roads and from Louisiana State University in Baton Rouge, Louisiana, with a major in history and minor in English. He is one of the few remaining speakers of Louisiana Creole French, having been immersed in childhood in the dialect spoken in Pointe Coupee Parish and is internationally regarded as an advocate of the Louisiana Creole people.

Wesley Morovic is a molecular microbiologist with a passion for unraveling the mysteries of genetics in biopharmaceuticals and life sciences. Graduating from the University of Wisconsin-Madison in 2006 with a bachelor's degree in biology, Wes has developed expertise in CRISPR-Cas genome editing, epigenetics, microbiology, and gene therapy, evidenced by his numerous peer-reviewed publications. He is currently enrolled in the master of business administration program at UW-Madison to help make gene and cell therapies more equitable. Beyond his scientific pursuits, Wes harbors a deep appreciation for history and believes that understanding our past is essential for building a brighter future. Wes is my oldest son and has been extremely helpful and supportive as I have written Daniel's book. He proofread and edited my manuscript and gave me lots of helpful suggestions. Mainly, his loving support is what kept me working on this book. Wes was born June 25, 1984, and now lives with his family in Edgerton, Wisconsin.

Gloria Moeller and Judy Birdsell were my co-workers at Freeport Junior High and in the early days of my research, they provided wonderful resources and support as I began searching for information about Daniel and the 46th Illinois.

Doug Evans, PhD, Captain, USN (retired), is the education committee chairman and member of the middle Tennessee speaker's bureau for the Tennessee Society Sons of the American Revolution. He gives presentations on Revolutionary War era history. He is also an active member of the Descendants of Valley Forge, Friends of Lafayette, and the Society of Cincinnati (Massachusetts). Doug is my high school classmate and good friend. He answered questions and edited parts of this book for me as well.

I would be remiss if I didn't mention my wonderful dogs who were my traveling companions on my numerous trips all over the country. They were always happy to hit the road and never complained when I spent extra time at places. Dakota is now with me, but the others have crossed the rainbow bridge: Buddy, Chanel, Kylie, and Shiloh all traveled with me throughout the years... not all of them at once though! I loved them all dearly.

References

Craib, Roderick. *A Picture History of U.S. Transportation: On Rails, Roads and Rivers*, Simmons-Boardman Publishing Corp., New York, 1958.

Chernow, Ron. *Grant*, Penguin Press, New York, 2017.

Civil War Diary of Simon M. Bott, Manuscripts Collection M-1156, Louisiana Research Collection, Howard-Tilton Memorial Library, Tulane University, New Orleans, LA 70118

Cooling, Benjamin Franklin. *Forts Henry and Donelson: The Key to the Confederate Heartland*. The University of Tennessee Press/Knoxville, 1987.

Cooling, Benjamin Franklin. *The Campaign for Fort Donelson: Civil War Series*, Eastern, National, 1999.

Costello, Brian J. *A History of Pointe Coupee Parish Louisiana*, Margaret Media, Inc. 2010.

Daniel, Larry J. *Shiloh: The Battle That Changed the Civil War*, Simon & Schuster, New York, 1997.

Davis, William C. *Brother Against Brother*, Time Life Books, 1983

Dayton, Aretas A. "The Raising of Union Forces in Illinois during the Civil War." *Journal of the Illinois State Historical Society (1908-1984)*, vol. 34, no. 4, 1941, pp. 401–438. JSTOR, www.jstor.org/stable/40189841. Accessed 27 Jan. 2020.

Emery, Tom. *The Civil War in Illinois*, 2014.

Helm, Gary. *Disease, Hunger, Death & Boredom, battlefields.org*

Hicken, Victor. *Illinois in the Civil War*, University of Illinois Press, 1991.

History of Stephenson County, County of Stephenson, Mrs. John W. Barrett, editor, Philip Keister, Mrs. John F. Woodhouse, editor, Freeport, 1972.

Hooper, Candice Shy. *"The Two Julias."* The New York Times, Disunion. February 14, 2013. Retrieved September 28, 2023.

Intravartolo, Cindy. *Journal of the Illinois State Historical Society (1998-)*, Vol. 107, No. 3-4 (Fall/Winter 2014), pp. 370-391.

Jones, Thomas B., 1841-; Dornblaser, Benjamin, 1828-1905. *Complete History of the 46th Regiment, Illinois Volunteer Infantry, A Full and Authentic Account of the Participation of the Regiment in the Battles, Sieges, Skirmishes and Expeditions in which it was Engaged*, W.H. Wagner & Sons, Freeport, 1907.

Letters of George Oscar Cooper, Soldier in the 46th Illinois.

McPherson, James M. *Battle Cry of Freedom: The Civil War Era*. Oxford University Press, Inc., 1988.

Ohland, Christopher. *A Brief History of the 46th Illinois Volunteer Infantry Regiment 1861-1866*, Second Edition, November 1995.

Parrotte, Emma E., "History of Camp Butler" (1938). Graduate Thesis Collection. 196. https://digitalcommons.butler.edu/grtheses/196

Parson, Thomas E. *Hell on the Hatchie*, Blue and Grey, 2007.

Tenney, W. J. *The Military and Naval History of the Rebellion in the United States*, 1865 & 1866.

Tomlinson, G. W., Banks, N. P. & J. Mayer & Co. (1863). *Tomlinson's Map of Port Hudson, Showing All of the Batteries, Strongholds, Principal Plantations &c.* [Boston, Mass.: G.W. Tomlinson] [Map] Retrieved from the Library of Congress, https://www.loc.gov/item/86691327/.

Vicksburg National Military Park Brochure, National Park Service, U.S. Department of the Interior, 2018.

Vicksburg: The Key to the South Booklet, Vicksburg Convention and Visitors Bureau, 2018.

Woodbury, Henry H. *Complete History of the 46th Illinois Veteran Volunteer Infantry*, Bailey & Ankney, Freeport, Illinois, 1866.

REFERENCES

Web Resources

dburgin.tripod.com/cw_xmas/cwarxmas2.html.

naucenter.as.virginia.edu/usct_odysseypart_2

legendsofamerica.com/il-cairo/2/

opinionator.blogs.nytimes.com/2012/10/26/brother-against-microbe/

bookwormhistory.com/2015/11/07/two-friends-a-river-hotel-and-the-legend-of-unconditional-surrender-grant-the-battle-of-fort-donelson/

ushistory.org/us/32d.asp

nps.gov/civilwar/search-battle-units-detail.htm?battleUnitCode=UUS0003RC00C

news.google.com/newspapers?nid=190&dat=19720113&id=Lx8jAAAAIBAJ&sjid=h0MDAAAAIBAJ&pg=6742,143156&hl=en

cem.va.gov/CEM/publications/NCA_Fed_Stewardship_Confed_Dead.pdf

usgwarchives.net/maps/tennessee/swtn1876.jpg?fbclid=IwAR0ey7_bFMLvX4CIjv3J4qY8mfcVnhgc4HWHEDQIO6xqYcgD9CFtJ0g48VM

georgetownsteamboats.com/gs/wp-content/uploads/2013/08/PowerShips2013Summer-p39.jpg

riverboatdaves.com/riverboats/p.html

www.ingramcontent.com/pod-product-compliance
Lightning Source LLC
Chambersburg PA
CBHW042138160426
43200CB00020B/2977